Quality First

KAISER

CHEVROLET

OLDSMOBILE
PRODUCT OF GENERAL MOTORS

BODY by FISHER

DODGE BROTHERS

PAIGE
The Standard of Value and Quality

AVBVRN

Automobile Book

THE SATURDAY EVENING POST
Automobile Book

The Curtis Publishing Company
Indianapolis, Indiana

Gil-Spear

Staff for The Saturday Evening Post Automobile Book
Jean White, Editor
Sandra Strother-Young, Art Director and Designer
Starkey Flythe, Jr., Editorial Director, Curtis Book Division
Jack Merritt, President, Curtis Book Division
David M. Price, Production Manager, Curtis Book Division
Jinny Sauer, Assistant Designer
Lucian Lupinski, Staff Artist
Astrid Henkels and Louise Fortson, Copy Staff
Marianne Sullivan, Dwight Lamb and Steve Miller,
Production and Art Assistants

Second Printing 1979

Contents

Through the Years

Cars on these two
pages are the 1939 Fords.
Above: the Ford V-8s, the
DeLuxe Ford V-8s, and the
Lincoln-Zephyr V-12s. Opposite page:
Mercury 8s, Lincoln V-12s
and a station wagon.

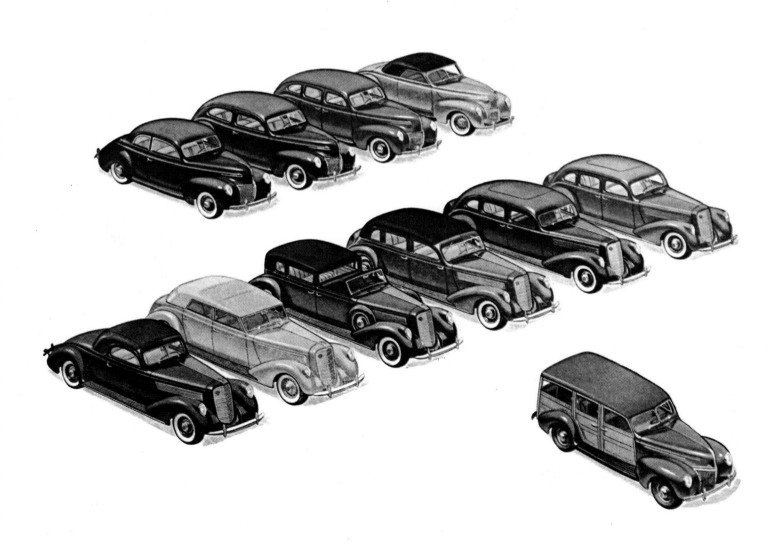

Through the Years

The automobile is as old as our century, and if the auto has changed in that space of time, so have we. Our clothing, our manners and morals, our attitudes—all have altered as profoundly as the design and engineering features of our vehicles. Take the swimsuit, for example. The costumes of these young ladies painted by Coles Phillips with a 1914 Overland were daring in their day. The following pages comprise a scrapbook of words and pictures from The Saturday Evening Post *to remind us of the way we were.*

The World Does Move

By Booth Tarkington, 1928

THERE WERE PEOPLE at that time (around 1900) who thought the automobile might be developed until someday it would become a vehicle of common use. A friend of mine even thought it would displace horses altogether.

"You'll live to see the day when there won't be any horses in the street and the horseless carriages are as ordinary as surreys are now," he said. But his prediction seemed to be fanciful. The machines were unreliable and the early enthusiasts who owned them led laborious and exasperated lives. They spent hours lying upon their backs in the street or in the mud or dust of country roads, striving with the inwards of perverse metals above them; they were never sure of arriving anywhere, or even of starting for anywhere. They often found themselves helpless at critical moments, and all moments were critical. They were mired in mud and had to hire horses; they hired horses on gentle hill slopes; they hired horses ignominiously in crowded streets; they bore conspicuous derision and sometimes

leaped for their lives from explosions, or from flames that encompassed them without warning.

The strange-shaped horseless grotesques were propelled by the action of steam or electricity, or explosive gas; there was conflict and argument over which served best, and there was further argument over what name the things should bear—"horseless carriages," or the French term "automobiles," or "cars," or just "machines." And when an attendant mechanic was hired, there was other debate upon a title for him. Should he be called "mechanic" or "mechanician" or "driver" or "chauffeur"? Mark Twain, with the many horse power of the elephant in mind, suggested "mahout."

When the gas machines moved they did it with outrageous uproar, and the vibration of them shocked the spines of the hardy experimentalists who rode in them. In 1903, in the early spring, I was stricken with typhoid fever, which harried me until the summer; and to soften the noises that came into the open windows of the sick room, the street was covered with fine sand to the depth of two inches for the distance of half a block. In the daytime no automobile would enter the sanded area; but sometimes, after dark, one that had not wandered into that shrouded street before would come chugging and snorting into the sand and be caught there like a fly in soft glue. Then there would be blasphemous metallic roarings, accompanied by simple human cursings, for half an hour perhaps.

But the new locomotion improved from month to month; engineers in creative frenzy designed and experimented; stranger and stranger new shapes clattered, banged and spat fire upon our streets; more horses ran away every day; and the upset citizens wrote fiercely to the papers demanding ordinances excluding motor-driven vehicles from the public highways. Nevertheless, the improvements went on, and in that same year, having added a sea voyage to a long convalescence, I drove from Brussels to Waterloo and back in a device called—by the attendant Italian mechanic—an automobilly, and was only slightly prostrated by the journey.

This automobilly was very high and shaped like an English brake; the engine howled in a ponderous box at the rear, and the front seat was protected by a tremulous leather dashboard from which one missed the whip socket. The driver steered with a bent rod, and the brave passengers mounted to their seats by means of a little stepladder which was afterward stowed away under the rear seat. The large wooden wheels had solid rubber tires, and their passage over an ancient stone-paved road would have been stimulating to the spinal ganglia if the performance by the engine's two large cylinders had not already attended to that. The return to Brussels was safely accomplished by four in the afternoon; the passengers walked into the hotel unaided; but having reached their rooms retired instantly to bed and did not rise again until noon of the next day.

Thereafter, for a time, we forswore horseless vehicles, let use them who would; they were intended evidently for people with rubber backbones and no fretful imaginations. When you were driving a horse and ran into anything, the impact of collision was with the force of a single steed, not thirty or forty; if you ran over a pedestrian, he endured the passing weight of some hundreds of pounds, not of several tons; if you ran over a dog, he got up and went home, terrified but usually not ruined. Moreover, if things went wrong when you were driving a horse, you had somebody to blame; a horse could hear what you said to him and be brought to repentance. You could never reform an automobilly or get any relief by abusing it.

Europe was beginning to use the machine nevertheless, and more of them were seen there than in America; they were improving more rapidly there than in America too; and in France we found that everybody talked about them excitedly.

"It's going to be a craze—and more," an elderly American who lived in Paris predicted one night at dinner. "It's going to be a craze on this side of the water first and then in America. It will be a craze in Europe first because of the splendid military highways and the improved roads generally. No sane person would attempt to do any touring in such machines on the horrible American roads; but when the craze becomes furious over there it may do a good thing; it may improve the roads so that one can drive about the country with horses in some comfort. Outside of that, I regard the self-moving vehicle as one of the most terrific visitations our old earth will ever endure."

Few lifetimes have spanned greater change than Booth Tarkington's, 1869–1946. He knew gleaming carriages and well-groomed horses, then the auto as an exciting novelty; finally, World War II and the A bomb.

"You're sure that a craze for the machine is coming?"

"It's in the air," he said. "Just now, to operate one of those outrages is the distinguished thing to do. Every few days one or another of my friends informs me that he has made the great investment. 'Well, I'm in for it!' he says, and his eyes glisten with pride and adventurous excitement. 'I have bought one!' Then he proceeds to boast of its horse power and swears that he has already driven it from Versailles to the Louvre in twenty-eight minutes. He has one hand in a bandage, a torn ear and a bruise over his eye, and he is delighted with these injuries. The women will help make it a craze because of the special costumes the sport requires—the wonderful hats, the veils, the pongee coats and gauntlets. And for the vanity of men, already it is a greater distinction to show automobile goggles sticking out of your breast pocket than a ribbon on your lapel. With these symptoms evident, the diagnosis is simple—within a very few years nobody's life will be safe the moment he steps out-of-doors."

"You aren't serious?"

"Try to cross the Champs Elysées when the crowd is returning from the Grand Prix," he said. "You will find that little task sufficiently preoccupying now, when all but a few of the vehicles are drawn by horses. Imagine the horse traffic complicated by great numbers of these roaring, darting machines. Of course I'm serious! *Les autos* are man's most dangerous invention, and I am not forgetting that his inventions have brought him the blessing of gunpowder and nitroglycerin. So far, the automobilists have contrived principally to get only themselves killed, and usually when they have been racing their dreadful contraptions; but as the craze spreads there will be massacres of innocents on every city boulevard and country highway. The new machine is simply a locomotive; but remember this mortal difference: A locomotive runs only upon the rails provided for it. Send

not a few but thousands of locomotives wandering irresponsibly over the face of Europe and America at a hundred kilometers an hour and you will have an idea of what this certainly coming contagion is going to do. And yet all the slaughter and destruction will be only a part of the curse that is to come upon the world."

The others at the table were amused by this prophesying, as preposterous as it was gloomy, and one of them asked, "What worse can a craze for horseless transport do than to massacre the innocents?"

"It can make a change in the life of the people," he said, not relaxing his gravity. "It will do more than mock the speed craze of the bicyclists; it will obliterate the accepted distances that are part of our daily lives. It will alter our daily relations to time, and that is to say it will alter our lives. Perhaps everybody doesn't comprehend how profoundly we are affected by such a change; but what alters our lives alters our thoughts; what alters our thoughts alters our characters; what alters our characters alters our ideals; and what alters our ideals alters our morals. When the horseless craze becomes universal it is not too much to say that the world will be inhabited by a new kind of people—and again I am serious."

"What kind of people will they be?"

"To themselves, they will of course represent an advance," he said. "They will look back upon us with a pitying contempt; but to us, as we are now, I think they would seem almost grotesque; they would appear to be machinery mad and strangely metallic. They will be unbelievably daring; they will be reckless of life—fast, materialistic, and yet incredibly prompt and efficient; therefore they will be richer than we are. Everything will be changed, because

Ads from the late '20s and early '30s suggest the speed-mad, materialistic world Tarkington predicted.

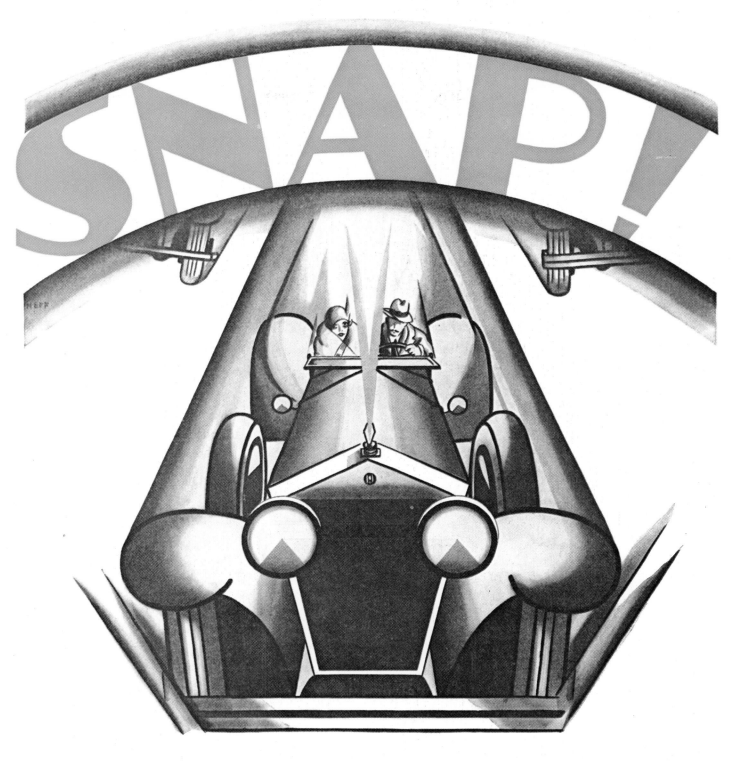

when a man accepts a new idea that revolutionizes his daily life, his mind becomes hospitable to every other new revolutionary idea. We are just entering the period when most of what we have regarded as permanently crystalline will become shockingly fluid—that is to say, we are already in the transition period between two epochs. We have seen the one and most of you here tonight will see something of the other. Your point of view will shift with the universal change; and, if you live, you will yourselves become strange inhabitants of the new world. A quarter of a century from tonight you will be taking as an accepted matter of course, and

without a shiver, things that are simply unthinkable to you now. And in the meantime, within only two or three years, every one of you will have yielded to the horseless craze and be the boastful owner of a metal demon; you will talk nothing but machines, and as you are being removed to the hospital you will babble to the stretcher-bearers of horsepower and kilometers per hour. Restfulness will have entirely disappeared from your lives; the quiet of the world is ending forever."

The pessimist gave us two or three years to begin our transfiguration into strange inhabitants of the new epoch but for my own part I did not need quite so long.

Like Tarkington's Lux, this 1899 Brenner could be entered via rear steps and door. Note the solid rubber tires.

The fair golden sunshine upon the boulevards became more and more shot with the blue vapors; the smell of burnt oil and gas grew tolerable to the nostrils and then actually enticing. Simultaneously, the trains to Paris from the country suburb where I had gone to live appeared to become more and more inconvenient until at last the day came when I perceived that the contagion was irretrievably upon me. Excited by the discovery of my condition, I lost no time but hurried to the office of an automobile agent on the Champs Elysées and asked him to be my friend. He had various kinds of automobiles to sell, on commission; I left it to him to choose which one was best suited to my circumstances and my ambitions.

The agent appeared to be a little puzzled by my request for his friendship; but, after looking at me thoughtfully for some moments, he said that nothing would give him greater pleasure. And when I explained that Providence had entirely denied me any talent for comprehending machinery, and that all I could ever hope to know about an automobile, through my own study and observation, was what color it had been painted, he became enthusiastic.

"You ask for my friendship," he said. "You shall have it; already I feel myself drawn to you. You need disinterested advice. Excellent! I am your friend and I will advise you. I have precisely what you want. I have a superb automobile for you. It is not entirely new; but that makes it all the better, because a little usage imparts elasticity to the operating devices. It has been owned by a friend of mine who feels himself compelled to part with it, though he has grown so fond of it that he will not give it up except to a person able to appreciate it. You will obtain a great deal of happiness from this superb vehicle. It is as fast as your heart could desire and the joy you will experience as you drive it at ninety or a hundred kilometers the hour——"

I interrupted him, though I liked what he was saying: "No; I—I don't think I'd better try to drive it myself. I have tried patiently to learn what makes these machines move, and I believe that I have succeeded in mastering the fundamental principle. My understanding is that an explosion of gas within a rigid compartment makes a pressure on something that is obliged to go up or down, or both, and this motion is somehow converted into a turning of wheels. Friends have tried to teach me how the motion is converted; they have drawn diagrams for me and I have faithfully studied them, but without any result whatever. To every mind there are certain things that cannot be conveyed, and this is one of the things that cannot be conveyed to mine. And as it seems to be established that unless one knows what takes place beneath one when one pushes a lever operating certain machinery over which one is sitting, one isn't justified in pushing such a lever, I have concluded that it will be safer for myself, and for people generally, so to speak, if I refrain from pushing the levers of this superb vehicle you have been so kind as to select for me. I think I should employ a chauffeur."

"Excellent!" the agent said. "But let me advise you, as your friend—first complete the purchase of the automobile we have selected. If you engage the chauffeur before you own the automobile, you will be embarrassed, because he would immediately ask you, 'What species of automobile am I expected to drive?' You would be confused and perhaps mortified to reply that you have no automobile. A certain amount of pretentiousness may attach to a person who, lacking an automobile, possesses a chauffeur."

"I hadn't thought of such a thing," I said hurriedly. "Could I see the automobile this morning?"

"Perfectly! Naturally you should see the automobile before you purchase it; but I tell you confidently you are going to be delighted. We will go at once." He took me to a garage and there displayed to me a red car which he patted proudly and affectionately. "Behold it! This is what I have promised you. Have you ever seen anything more perfectly fitted to your special requirements? Think how you will look in it in the Bois de Boulogne! And observe, you will not need to buy any equipment or accessories except some tools. It already has a covering, which can be elevated in case of rain, and two splendid oil lamps with reflectors; you will not be annoyed by having to purchase a top and lamps, nor by the delay of getting them fitted to the machine; they are included in the price. Did I not tell you it is superb?"

Some workmen had joined us and I wished to appear intelligent. "What horse power has it?" I asked.

"Forty—forty horses would be needed to do what it will do."

"Ah—what kind of a car is it?"

"What kind? It is a touring car."

"I mean what make."

"It is Italian, a magnificent Lux."

"Is it, indeed?" I said, impressed. "A genuine Lux?"

"Genuine? It could not be more so. Observe it!"

I did. I went to it and looked at it carefully. There was a narrow door in the middle of the rear wall for the

Special headgear was de rigueur *in the early days—caps and goggles for men, broad-brimmed hats swathed in veiling for women.*

entrance of passengers, and when this door was closed a little seat could be swung down from it, thus allowing three people to sit in the tonneau. Moreover, a long wicker hamper was strapped to each side of the car, above the rear wheels, and these arrangements pleased me.

"It is very convenient," I said. "People can get in by the little door and these hampers seem to me a great improvement. Luncheon could be carried in them, or almost anything."

"Yes," the agent agreed; "luncheon, maps, an umbrella, a cane—anything you wish. I was sure you would be delighted with the baskets. Are they not charming? As you say, they are a great improvement, and only a few of the very finest automobiles are equipped with them. Every convenience you can imagine accompanies this superb Lux. Have I been correct? This is perfectly the car you wish to buy?"

"I—I think so. I believe——"

One of the mechanics who stood by interrupted. "Don't you care to look at the engine?"

"Indeed, I do," I said. "Where is it?"

"It is in front," the agent explained. "All the most modern automobiles have the engine in front under a protecting hood nowadays." He opened the hood. "Observe it! Have you ever beheld a more perfect mechanism? Isn't it a masterpiece?"

"I'm sure it must be," I said. "Could we take a drive?"

"A drive?" he repeated thoughtfully. "A drive?"

He spoke to two of the workmen and withdrew with them to a corner of the garage, where the three engaged in a long conversation, gesticulating earnestly, while I again examined the baskets and the little door, becoming more and more pleased with them. Finally the agent returned to me.

"You shall have your drive," he said benevolently. "First, we shall go to lunch; after that we shall come back and then you shall have your drive."

When we came back, we climbed into the car

through the fascinating little door and sat in the tonneau, while a serious-looking mechanic occupied the driver's seat and another went to the crank in front of the car to start the engine. The agent chatted gaily, speaking often of the charming wicker hampers; but the seriousness of the workman who was to drive appeared to increase, and so did that of his companion, who was for some time violently engaged with the crank.

"Do not be discouraged," the agent said. "Often the best of automobiles—even a Lux—will require several turns of the crank before the engine——"

He was interrupted by a shattering roar; the engine had gone into action and the mechanic leaped back from the crank, then climbed into the seat beside the driver.

"Do not be disturbed," the agent shouted in my ear. "The noise is rather loud because we are in an inclosure. In the open, you will almost not notice it at all. Also, there will be much less vibration as soon as we are in motion."

When we were out of doors I persuaded myself that he was correct. We sounded like an itinerant battle and we undeniably vibrated; but we moved with startling rapidity, the wind hard in our faces; and I found the experience so exciting, even so exhilarating, that when we returned I decided that this superb Lux must be mine. I had a final moment of hesitation.

"You remember," I said to the agent, "you said you would act as my friend, my trusted adviser. I appeal to you now as you stand in that capacity. Do you sincerely advise me to buy this automobile from you?"

He looked me in the eye. "I will reassure you," he said earnestly and gently. "Listen well to what I am going to tell you. It is simply this: I give you my word of honor that I would sell this automobile to my own brother."

That settled it. I signed the purchase papers on the spot; but when I engaged a chauffeur and we attempted to take the superb Lux home, I began to comprehend that the agent's brother, at some time in their lives, had done him a horrible injury. . . .

DRAWN BY EDWARD PENFIELD

In 1905 Post *cover artist Guernsey Moore, who had been painting beautiful girls with fine horses, began to paint beautiful girls in sporty autos.*

The World and the Automobile

Editorial, 1902

Is THE AUTOMOBILING CRAZE going to pass through the same course that the bicycle epidemic did, and if so, when will its culminating point be reached? This without regard to the vehicle's utilitarian employment, but simply with respect to its use as an implement of outdoor sport and a visible evidence that its owner knows the proper thing to do and has the price to do it. Certainly the turning point will not be reached this year; but what of next year, or the year after? This thing can't go on always; other things may—nay, are—hanging over us by a single hair—say, flying machines.

But a more interesting consideration is the practical side of auto-locomotion. That the automobile as a vehicle for human nature's daily use is here to stay cannot be doubted. Thousands are in use solely because they are found preferable to horse-propelled vehicles. As delivery wagons for the larger stores, and as used by the express companies, they are becoming common in all

Flat tires were a frequent occurrence in 1902, when country roads were strewn with horseshoe nails, and it was nice to have a chauffeur along to make repairs. To set a rubber patch on a damaged inner tube you used a portable vulcanizer that burned gasoline—many motorists had singed eyebrows.

cities. The smaller tradesmen—the grocers and butchers—must soon find it profitable to employ them. When this comes about the observing student of urban affairs will watch curiously to see if the butcher boys drive theirs twice as fast as the grocerymen, since he, the observing student, has long noted that butcher carts always proceed at something like double the speed of grocery wagons.

It is said that the commercial possibilities of auto-locomotion are only just beginning to be realized. Sanguine persons, their fancy perhaps auto-propelled, predict that railroad trains, both freight and passenger, are to be superseded by auto-vehicles of various styles. Already auto-sleighs are in use in Russia, and an Italian prince is said to have ordered one of substantial build in which he will make an attempt to reach the North Pole. The plain citizen may be permitted to observe that the prince will find the Polar roads in rather poor condition. He will also learn that it is impracticable to replenish his larder with chunks of raw auto-sleigh, a point in which the time-honored dog-team has an immeasurable advantage.

But perhaps the most daring thing in automobiles is one for use in the African deserts now being

1903 Searchmont

1903 Rambler

Never on Sunday—until the motorcar set Americans free to enjoy the great out-of-doors on weekends. The farm or carriage horse worked during the week and had to be allowed to rest on Sundays. Not so the family auto, which made possible Sunday outings like this 1905 picnic.

constructed by French inventors. It will have a boat-shaped body of aluminum, with a screw at the rear, and when it comes to a river it will plunge in and propel itself across. The little difficulty of a mountain is arranged for by a capstan and rope by which it will pull itself up the steepest incline. No doubt if pursued by a lion it can climb a tree, but the person who maintains that it can and will pull the tree up after it, goes too far; it will do nothing of the sort: after the lion has gone away it will let itself down and proceed onward as if nothing had happened.

The ingenious promoter of this African affair professes to believe that his invention will do away with the use of camels. This may be, though one not possessed of stock in his company scarcely looks to see the ship of the desert become a drug on the market immediately. If the desert autos are going to penetrate many leagues into the interior the question of fuel may arise. An automobile, no matter how many screws and capstans it may have, will never command respect with a caravan of two dozen camels following, each loaded with four barrels of gasoline. Nor will the Italian prince be taken seriously if he starts off with a score of well-fattened dogs tied behind.

1905 Winton

1906 Reo

The first of many Post *covers celebrating the plight of the beautiful girl whose car has broken down appeared in 1906.*

A Race Through the Night

By Hamblen Sears, 1903

Eleanor Marsten is the heroine of "The Retroactive Wager," a story that appeared in the Post in 1903 when it was taken for granted that a gently bred lady would hate motorcars ("ugly machines with filthy-smelling engines") and fear traveling faster than a carriage horse could trot.

Late one evening Eleanor pretends to receive a telegram indicating her father has met with an accident at a hotel 60 miles from where she is visiting friends. It is urgent that she

hurry to his side, she says, but there is no train until morning. Friends arrange for wealthy sportsman Stanley Gardner to drive Eleanor there in his powerful racing machine.

TWENTY MINUTES LATER the huge machine with its two acetylene eyes stopped at the door.

"Don't try too much speed, Stan," called Jim, as he and his wife watched the searchlights spring from tree to tree as the machine moved out of the avenue.

They were on the road in a few moments. Then Stanley turned to Miss Marsten. "Listen carefully, now, please. Hold hard with this hand—so—now take hold of this bulb—that's it—press it"—a hoarse note sounded—"and again. Keep pressing that every few seconds. If anything goes wrong touch my arm. I can't pay any attention to you at all. Can you stand it?"

"Yes," said a voice that vibrated with emotion.

"Will you stop me if I go too fast?"

"Yes. But please go—Oh, won't you get me there?"

"Never fear, Miss Marsten," he answered grimly. "I'll get you there or bust."

The car jumped forward an instant; then again to a faster speed; and then with a wild whirr it seemed to fly from a stationary position as he pushed the lever forward to the fourth gear. The man leaned low over his wheel with his eyes fastened on the stretch of road that showed before the lamps. The girl crouched against him involuntarily.

A hand suddenly closed over hers in the darkness; lifted it and placed it on the horn bulb. Immediately she remembered and began squeezing it, her eyes fixed on the bright spot of road, too. Everywhere, all else was blackness. Suddenly into the light rushed something and after it was gone she remembered that it was a cart with one horse. There appeared to be no wind, no noise, no light nor darkness—nothing on earth but that white streak of road, always the same, into which flew a house, a fence, a tree, a cart that

Stanley grips the wheel; Eleanor grips her 1903 hat.

was gone before it could be recognized or placed in her brain. It seemed as if she could not stand the strange silence. There was no world except within the car. There was nothing behind, only always something unknown in front—the strange, fascinating chance of something that might come into that white area and for once be dead ahead instead of on one side. It seemed as if she could not bear it. She wanted to cry out—she did.

"Do I blow hard enough?"

The round-shouldered figure beside her never moved.

She touched his arm almost unconsciously.

Instantly the brake went down, the power off, and the hot monster came to a panting rest so suddenly that it threw her forward on the motor.

"Oh!" cried the girl.

"What is it?" asked Stanley sharply.

"Why—why—I don't know—I wondered if I blew the horn often enough."

"What's the real trouble?" he demanded.

"I don't know—I think"—and she turned her veiled face to him—"I think I was lonely. Can't you—er—talk?"

"Talk! Why, good Heavens, girl, if there was the least turn of this wheel—the least bit of slippery road—any kind of man, woman, child, cart—anything coming along, we would"—and he laughed hoarsely—"we'd never know what hit us." She shuddered. "But don't you worry. Keep on blowing the horn. Now, look out!" And the huge monster flew on again through the night, rattling and wheezing, and giving forth a hoarse cry under the pressure of a young girl's hand.

Suddenly a hand grasped hers and held the horn; Stanley straightened in his seat, turned his ear forward, and sat still as they flew along. She did not move and in a moment he released her hand. In a dull way she wondered why he did it—and they flew over a railroad crossing.

A light or two appeared in the black wall which only their lanterns pierced—the crank moved —they slowed down, and then seemed to fly through a little village.

Darkness again, and the same dread of the loneliness and the black, silent, hunch-backed figure beside her. The machine slowed, stopped; Gardner got out.

"What is it?" whispered the terrified girl.

"Spark's working bad," he muttered.

"Oh!" said she, understanding nothing.

She watched six minutes tick off the clock. "Where are we?" she asked.

"Just outside Woodville," he answered from the front of the car. Then as he got in again, "Hold hard, now. We've got a perfectly level road for nearly all the rest of the way."

With a touch of the crank and a word of encouragement to her they were off again. The two bent forward, the horn screamed on through the night, and nothing but the fascination of that stream of light interested her until many lights showed far ahead and he slowed down to a speed that seemed like crawling. She turned to him. Before she could even congratulate herself on being through with it they pulled up at the steps of the hotel.

Note: the distance traveled was 60 miles; the elapsed time 1 hour, 53 minutes. That averages out to only about 30 mph, but that was fast enough in 1903, after dark, on roads designed for horse-drawn traffic.

Speeders were called "scorchers" in the early days. These drive a 1916 Oldsmobile.

The Speed Maniac

Editorial, 1907

THE OTHER AFTERNOON, while going along a narrow but excellent road, I heard the hum of an approaching car, which I could not see because of the dust about it. As I never take chances when others are with me, I gave up the entire roadbed, running my car slowly, and had only just cleared when there flashed past in the middle of the road, and with such a dust cloud all around him that the driver could not possibly see twenty feet ahead, a racer, runabout type, going at the rate of probably fifty miles an hour!

The driver was bent over the wheel, the woman with him was doubled in an effort to keep on her hat and escape the bewildering dust, neither of them could possibly see, as I say, twenty feet ahead, and yet they were going along, keeping the middle of the road, sounding no horn, and at the rate of fifty miles an hour!

If I had not got entirely off the road, no doubt there would have been coffins for several. Now, is any punishment too severe for a driver of that kind?

At his best, the automobilist is a considerate gentleman who slows down and sounds his horn on coming to a crossroad, who invariably notifies a driver of his approach by a small toot of the horn, who crowds neither pedestrians nor wagons into the ditch or so near to it that they are in danger of falling, who obeys the request to "slow down" and who does not shower with mud and water people he chances to have overtaken just at a pool, or confuse with his approach and dust those he may have come upon in a turn of the road. In a word, he is considerate of the rights of those he meets, and it is entirely from that viewpoint that I write.

Intelligent people do not offer objection to the speeding of automobiles, if the increased pace ceases through

Wake! For the Car that scatters into flight
The Hens before it in a flapping Fright,
Drives straight up to your Door, and
bids you Come
Out for a Morning Hour of Sheer Delight.

We are no other than a Moving Row
Of Automobile Cranks that come and go.
And what with Goggles and
Talc-windowed Veils,
In Motoring Get-up, we're a Holy Show!

Carolyn Wells, 1906

Hold onto your hats! A 1908 advertisement for the Franklin stressed "reliable automobiling 365 days a year" since there was no water-filled radiator to freeze in winter. The motor was air-cooled—and so were the passengers! Price: $4,000 for the 42 h.p., six-cylinder touring car.

towns and on such roads where the request to reduce speed is made; intelligent people realize that the automobile is a great stride in methods of transportation; that, from being a luxury, it has now come almost to be a necessity; that it has come to stay, and that its requirements must be fairly considered in legislation. It is not fair to place speed limits at unnecessarily low figures; they should be put at such figures as is necessary to safeguard the ordinary traffic of the road. Once such a figure is established, however (and ten miles the hour is generally agreed to meet the sane judgment of all), compliance should be exacted under penalty of jail, instead of a fine, which has very little, if any, deterring effect upon the class of automobile owners that supplies the flagrant offenders of not only local speed regulations, but of the common rules of decency.

For the farmer and his wife, life changed overnight. They were no longer isolated from the amenities—or the economic opportunities—of town and city.

The Farmer and His Motorcar

Anonymous, 1909

A NEW BUYER has entered the automobile field—the well-to-do farmer. When he comes to town on Saturday he looks longingly at the shiny motorcars lined up in the dealer's garage and finally edges around to the man in a leather cap with: "What do they cost?" Then he does some figuring: "Let's see, eleven hundred bushels of wheat at ninety-three cents, ten hundred and twenty-three dollars, enough to buy one—and I raised it on thirty-seven acres. Or eleven head of steers at ninety dollars—and I have fifty of them ready for market. Why not use some of my property and have a little enjoyment in this world?"

So he thinks in terms of products and, as a result, the

The farmer could rush his produce to city markets, or he could sell it at roadside to motorists who swarmed out into the country on weekends.

salesmen in the interior towns have a new list of possible customers. They are shrewd customers, too. It requires skill to sell a thousand-dollar vehicle to a man whose notion of luxury has been measured by a seventy-five-dollar, rubber-tired buggy. . . .

The level roads of the prairie States from Indiana west to the Rocky Mountains are exceedingly favorable to farmer ownership of motors. In Iowa's agricultural college a short winter course in instruction in the theory and use of the gasoline motor was given the past winter.

The students were, as a preliminary, taught the structure and operation of gasoline engines, and learned the many ways in which such an engine can be made use of to make farming easier and more profitable. They were instructed in the dismantling, rebuilding and operation of motorcars, so that they might become skilled operators of such vehicles, which, the State educational authorities are convinced, will perform a large part in the development of the farming interests in the next two decades.

All smiles! Every member of the family shared pride in ownership of the wonderful vehicle that conferred mobility on rural America. Opposite, Mead Schaeffer portrayed farmers' vehicles outside a country church during New Year's Eve service for the cover of the December 30, 1944, Post.

"Can I take care of a car and keep it going?" is another question from the farmer that the dealer must answer. At first some of the buyers do not succeed in management. Three hours after a purchaser had left a small town garage with his new motor the rural telephone called the salesman. "What makes the water boil so in my radiator? And the automobile"—the farmer likes to say automobile—"runs so slow. It climbs hills all right, but doesn't make time."

The agent was puzzled for a minute. Then he asked: "Did you change the speed levers any after leaving the garage?" "No, I didn't touch anything except the little irons on the wheel." That accounted for it—he had run seven miles on low gear!

The family of the farmer who owns a car enjoys more pleasure, sees more attractions of town, and gets more out of life. At the Sunday afternoon gathering at the country church, at the country wedding, at the public auction—everywhere, except at funerals—are motorcars standing among the wagons and buggies, showing how multiplied is their use. . . .

The farmer seized quickly on the telephone and made it his own. He has put into his house bathtubs, lighting plants, pianos and phonographs. He has awakened to good roads and is wedded to the rural delivery. His horses have, for the most part, become so accustomed to motorcars that accidents are rare. As he sees seventeen-year-old boys and girls acting as chauffeurs, he has made up his mind that he is entitled to his share of the enjoyment. With this attitude toward the swift machines, the dealer has a simplified proposition and his sales will increase as months go by.

One-Tenth Done

Editorial, 1915

THERE were just above twenty million families in the United States at the last census. To be sure, a census family is a rather scandalous statistical invention, for it includes all those who share a common abode. Thus, a railroad construction gang sleeping in a box car is a statistical family; but, by and large, the number of families thus enumerated differs only slightly from natural families, and we may take twenty millions as the measure of families in the ordinary sense in 1910.

In the fiscal year that ended with June, six hundred and sixty thousand passenger automobiles were sold in the United States for considerably more than half a billion dollars; and this brings the total registration of automobiles in the country to just above two millions.

Six hundred and sixty thousand cars in a year that included eleven months of world's war and was characterized by abnormal business throughout, looks, at first glance, like a good many; and amateur economists who think cars are good for them, but bad for farmers, are welcome to such strictures as may occur to them.

The main point is that, with twenty million families and only two million automobiles, we have got our national job one-tenth done. When every family has an automobile we can take some credit to ourselves.

Cars were easier to drive and easier to buy after 1912, when Cadillac introduced the self-starter and Studebaker announced the first installment buying plan. By 1916 Henry Ford's low-priced cars accounted for 45 percent of all sales, though magazines carried more advertising for makes like Overland (above), manufactured 1903-1908 in Indianapolis and 1908-1927 in Toledo, and the Mitchell, manufactured 1903-1923 in Racine, Wisconsin. Opposite, a 1914 ad for dress patterns.

Much early automobile advertising enumerated technical features or claims regarding economy or dependability. These Oldsmobile ads from 1907 (above) and 1908 (below) are among the first to portray the auto as a status symbol. The message, never put into words: "Our car is at home in scenes of elegance and sophistication where people wear the height of fashion." (In the car below a pet dog wears goggles.) We can be grateful that this kind of advertising art proliferated in the '20s and '30s. It delights the eye.

The Auto Thieves

By Arthur Train, 1915

TIME WAS when the brains of the criminal élite were studiously devoted to the cracking of safes; then came the era of the porch climber and second-story men; and finally, strong-arm work having become unprofitable owing to the increased efficiency of the police, politer forms of crime became popular, and the crook laid aside the dark lantern and the slung shot in favor of the forger's pen and the glittering stock certificate of the fake promoter. Yet it is not so far a cry from the days of the holdup to the present, for with all the world awheel the daring bravado of the old days seems to have come again into its own, even on little old Broadway, and the horse thief to have been reincarnated in the motor crook.

It did not take thieves long to discover that a motor is the easiest thing in the world to steal. It is worth stealing, to begin with; its identity can be almost destroyed in a few hours, and it merrily whirls itself and the thief away to safety and concealment at fifty miles an hour. Then began, for a while, the heyday of a crime for which law enforcement officials were unprepared.

Things reached a point where a man's motor would disappear while he was in the drugstore, drinking an innocent glass of soda water, or during any other brief interval in which the motor might be left unguarded. Sometimes half a dozen would be taken in one day, and there was one case on record where the president of an automobile company had driven up to the door of his showroom on Broadway, only to have his motor stolen behind his back as he stood on the threshold talking to one of his employees. It almost seemed as if the cars ran away of their own accord. One chauffeur complained that his car had suddenly begun to move as he was engaged in lighting the tail lamp, and had shot down the street into the dusk, never to be seen again. It was almost impossible to trace the thieves.

A typical case would be something like this: Dr. Rufus Jones—who, we will suppose, rather fancies himself as a mechanic, is a general motor fan and drives his own car—receives a hurry call to visit an unknown patient at an apartment house uptown. He goes there, finds the party lives on the top floor, and climbs seven flights of stairs, leaving his motor at the curb. When he arrives at the flat he discovers that the patient knows nothing of the call; in fact, never heard of the doctor. In a word, it is a fake call. Indignantly he descends to the street, having been gone, say, six minutes, to find that his new little town car has vanished. The doctor notifies the nearest police station, calls up headquarters, and watches anxiously every motor that whirs by. But he never sees his car again. Why? Because it is now in Fall River, its engine and serial number altered, and the body painted a bright baby-blue. Depending on circumstances, the transformation has occurred either in a New York garage, a barn in the suburbs, Hartford, or even Fall River itself. The chances are 95 percent in favor of the owner's not recovering it. How can he? Once outside the immediate vicinity of the good doctor's office, who is to recognize the fact that the motor is a stolen motor or the youth who is driving it a thief?

Chalmers was one of many proud names that disappeared during the shake-out decade of the '20s, when 161 automobile companies closed their doors forever. Chalmers had been merged with Maxwell and Walter P. Chrysler was in charge when, in 1923, he decided to jettison the old name and bring out a new make with his own name on it. The 1916 models shown here ranged in price from $1,090 for the touring car above to $2,480 for the town car opposite.

The Lady Duff-Gordon who lent her name to Chalmers advertising is best remembered for the supporting role she played in one of the great dramas of the age, the sinking of the Titanic in 1912. Together with her husband and her secretary she climbed into Lifeboat No. 1 which pulled away from the sinking ship with only 12 persons in space intended for 40. About 1,500 persons drowned while Lifeboat No. 1 awaited rescue at a discreet distance. Lady Duff-Gordon remembered later that at the moment the great ship slid beneath the sea she was consoling her secretary for the loss of a beautiful nightgown left aboard.

Interior by Lady Duff-Gordon

Automobile Advertisement, 1916

I HAVE BEEN ENGAGED by the Chalmers Motor Company to select materials for furnishing the interiors of their new closed cars.

As for myself—I am not interested in the exterior of this Chalmers town car. If external things interest you, glance at the picture.

Neither am I concerned in the least with the motor. I know not and care not whether it be what mechanical men call a six, a 22, or a 3400. *Les détails m'ennuie.* I leave them to Monsieur Chauffeur.

My only interest is in the vitally important thing— the interior. All important because there is where I have to sit. It is my sun-parlor on wheels, and if colors clash or upholstery fabric grates on my nerves, how am I to love the car?

Nothing can recompense for poor taste.

When the Chalmers designers came to me for advice on their closed cars I was a bit doubtful of being able to please everyone of the hundreds of people who will buy Chalmers Sedans, town cars and limousines this year. To please everyone, when there are so many diversified tastes, seemed difficult.

But when I saw assembled the vast assortment of handsome fabrics, silks, carpets and cords, my spirits rose to the task.

I have tried above all to make the cars livable. That undoubtedly will be your first impression of this town car. It is thoroughly and unqualifiedly livable.

The woodwork is of inlaid mahogany; the floors richly carpeted.

Windows are silk curtained. There's a lounging pillow of eiderdown and silk, a dainty hassock. And the soft harmonious colorings make the picture utterly complete and a delight to the eye, viewed from the inside or whizzing past the curb.

A toilette for milady was by no means forgotten. And it is unnecessary to mention such conveniences as electric dome lamps, a clock, a robe rail and chofone speaking tube.

Press a little button, and a smoking set or the dainty toilette case springs out from concealment.

That is quite enough of detail. The colors—they are what I really intended to discuss. But after all, how fruitless it is to try to describe superb colorings. I shall resign the task, not only because it is impossible, but because I do not want to spoil your first impression of the car by a premature description of the color blendings.

Although this is my first experience in costuming a motor carriage, I am immensely pleased with the final result.

And I can say, regarding the interior of this town car, I believe 'twill please you.

Lucy Duff Gordon

The Motor Truck Goes to War

By Edward Hungerford, 1918

A MAN stood beside a highroad, outside the French city of Bar-le-Duc, on a spring morning and watched the motor trucks go rolling up to Verdun. The road was an old one, and a famous one as well; the Sacred Way, the folk of the neighborhood had named it long years before, yet it never had really earned that appellation until the spring of 1916. For the Crown Prince was hammering at the defenses of Verdun, feverishly but impotently, while the motor trucks that an observer saw rolling out of Bar-le-Duc day after day on those spring mornings were bringing succor and supplies to the blue-coated men of the garrison, which will go down into history as the modern pass of Thermopylae.

It is thirty-four miles from Bar-le-Duc up to Verdun by the national highway; in time of peace a little more than forty by rail. The best train on the Meuse Valley Railroad—freely translated from the official guide of the French *chemins de fer*—does the run in two hours to the minute. But the poor little Meuse Valley Railroad long since has been cast into oblivion. A network of defense and enemy trenches crosses and recrosses its right-of-way, and it has ceased to exist. And France's main pathway—almost the sole pathway—up to her great fortress was a highroad; her dependence, the motor-truck transport upon that highroad.

The man—he was an American—who stood by the Sacred Way saw that the trucks came in even companies, ten deep and in single file. He had noticed on other roads the tendency of the French military authorities to run their rams, or sections of trucks, ten deep—a practice which has now been adopted by our own authorities for the United States military transport service over there. On some of these roads and on occasion the French motor trucks had run four abreast as well. The entire road had been set aside for one-way

Entering World War I late, the U.S. profited by the experience of the Allies and avoided all use of horses. Truck manufacturers cooperated to produce just one standardized model, the Liberty truck, which proved enormously useful behind the battle lines in France.

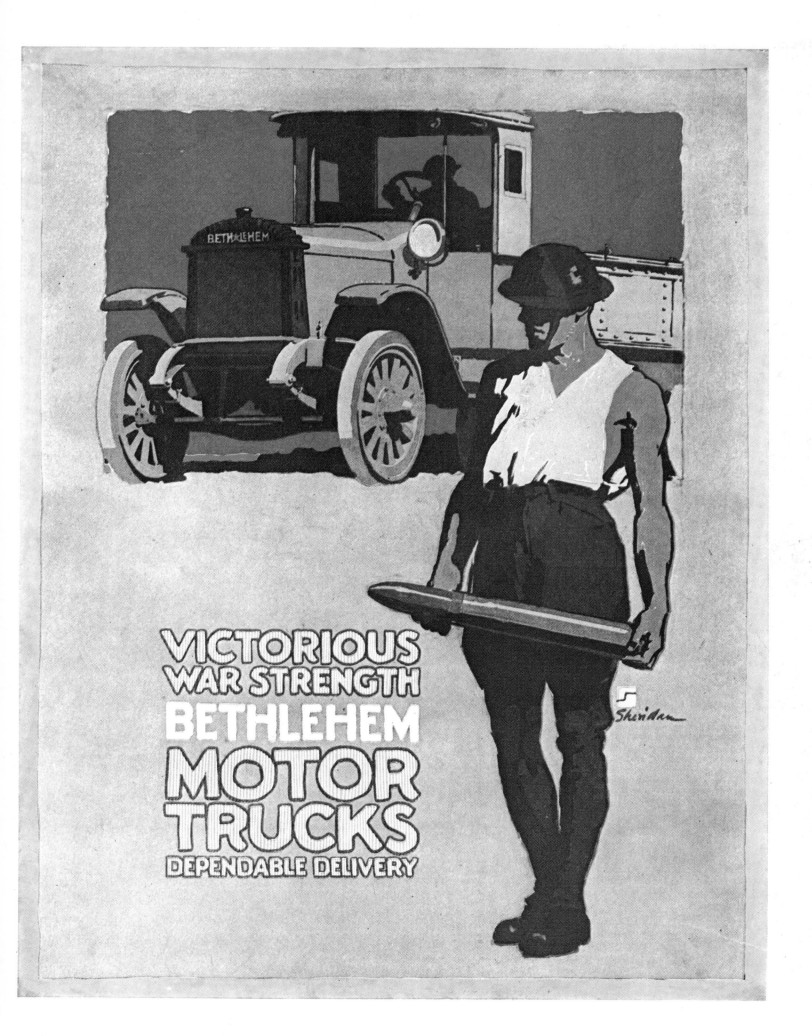

VICTORIOUS WAR STRENGTH
BETHLEHEM
MOTOR TRUCKS
DEPENDABLE DELIVERY

traffic, and upon its paved surface—thirty-two feet from curb to curb—four trucks had proceeded side by side—a neat trick of driving when one considers that each of the trucks had a width over all of exactly seven feet.

On the road to Verdun nothing of that complicated sort was attempted. For one thing it was considerably narrower—classed as but a third-class road upon the military maps of the French—and not wide enough for even three vehicles abreast. Moreover, it was compelled to take care of the returning traffic. What goes up must

come down. And though it is better that it should go up one road and come down the other, at Verdun, standing like a headland out among the angry breakers of the enemy, that was quite out of the question. The Sacred Way was forced to bear the burden of the traffic in both directions.

It was given every possible assistance for the bearing of this burden. During the days of its great task horse-drawn traffic and passenger motors of every sort were rigidly barred from it. A system of traffic police as inflexible as the statuesque figures on Fifth Avenue, New York, enforced the strict rules of the road. And the entire traffic movement was in control of a competent military officer, who, with a telephone affixed to his ear, ruled the situation like the train dispatcher of a busy railroad. The rams went forward at an even rate of nine and a half miles an hour. The ten trucks of a single ram were spaced at a regular distance of ten to fifteen yards. The last of the ten carried at its rear a huge red disk. This, interpreted, meant that the first truck of the succeeding ram must not approach within fifty yards. This longer space gave opportunity for the swift cars or motorcycles of the officers in charge of the steady flow of men and munitions to slip ahead of the slow, steadily moving column whenever it was necessary. They never broke between the units of the single ram. And when the traffic police along the road found it necessary to hold up or split the column they did it between the rams. The red disks were their aid.

Slow work but sure. And not always so very slow at that. A single army corps was moved up from back of Bar-le-Duc to Verdun in less than ten hours. It was an impressive sight—truck upon truck—every twenty-fifth one a kitchen, and every fiftieth a workshop. And almost all the others filled with soldiers—soldiers who after five months of heavy fighting compelled the young whelp of the Hohenzollerns to give a new respect to Verdun and the things for which Verdun stands. And while these were going up the road most of those returning were also filled—with worn and wounded soldiers, with the retiring civilian population of Verdun and such of its furniture and personal effects as could be packed and moved in small space. The double procession was continuous. Nothing was permitted to delay or hinder it seriously. If a truck broke down and could not be repaired and sent forward at normal speed within sixty seconds, it was crowded into the ditch and for the time being abandoned. Then, at intervals of a few days and whenever the military situation so permitted, the road was entirely closed to ordinary traffic and salvage corps went forward to clean up the wreckage.

In this way the motor truck played its part in the salvation of Verdun—and no small part it was.

The year: 1917. The place: the main street of Sauk Centre, Minnesota, later famous as Main Street. *The tourists: Sinclair and Grace Hegger Lewis. Note camping gear bundled on running board and in the rear seat. The first Mrs. Lewis wears her khaki riding costume; "Red" is dressed more nattily, perhaps because it's his hometown.*

Adventures in Automobumming

By Sinclair Lewis, 1919

IN THE GOOD OLD DAYS, when the happy citizenry were not annoyed by bathtubs, telephones or having enough to eat, any lad could get a deal of innocent pleasure, before he settled down to growing the rest of his beard, out of becoming a pirate and collecting pieces of eight, burning monasteries and torturing old women. Nowadays, fiction writers assure us, there is no chance for a man with courage and imagination to go freely roving the world.

Yet the coming of the gasoline motor, whether in a flivver with a delivery-wagon body or in a tranquil twelve, has brought back the age of joyous piracy, with the immense advantage that you do not have to associate with pirates who have the absentminded habit of cutting your throat. The long-distance motor tourist, swooping down a corkscrew hill into a shining white town of which he has never heard, sliding along a ridge with the fields to westward droning in blue shadows, picking up a wayfarer with a new dialect and a new world of interests, is adventurous as any heaving brigantine wallowing all day through changeless seas. He is far more independent—he doesn't have to stay on that uncomfortable and highly undependable medium, the ocean, which is so notoriously ill-suited to walking back after the ship gets wrecked.

Out on the ribbed prairies a lone car really looks like a craft on the circle of the ocean. And as to the practical side of piracy—if the driver doesn't care to attend to that himself he can have it satisfactorily performed by mechanics, hotel keepers and lunchroom cooks along the way.

They who have escaped the touring habit usually ask what is necessary for a long trip. Must they take tents, a pile of extra casings, a seven-foot atlas, a grand piano and a vacuum cleaner? Must they be combinations of aviators, deep-sea divers and Dan'l Boones to essay a whole five hundred miles from home?

These Model T-era auto tourists may have read Sinclair Lewis's articles in the Post *and been inspired to try "automobumming" for themselves.*

They may take all the equipment they desire, but the fact is that a respectable citizen with a second-hand flivver, who has never driven any car for more than a hundred miles, can start on twenty minutes' notice—ten for his wife to buy a hairnet, ten to tell the maid what she mustn't let the baby do—and with safety and not much trouble hike from Miami to Seattle. He will find repairmen every five miles most of the distance; lingerie can be washed in roadside brooks; and from corner to corner of the country run through trails with markers on telephone poles at every turn.

If he wants to camp no one will examine him for insanity. All schoolteachers expect to have to crawl between rolls of red comforters and piles of frying pans when they reach their school yards; and any modern farmer would feel lonely if he didn't glance out of the peacock room in the morning and see on the front steps a car that was a combination dining room, nursery and xylophone.

But the motor trip is to be considered not merely as a vacation but as a duty for all conscientious citizens, for there is nothing which so swiftly and painlessly reduces swellings of the head.

The average citizen never thinks he is an average citizen. Whether he is an insurance man, a fishmonger, a writer of fiction or a trick balloonist, he believes that he is extremely necessary to his business and to his home. He knows at least two people who ask his advice and he expects the corner bootblack to call him "Boss." His grocer remembers his favorite brand of tomatoes and the washerwoman is still grateful because of the derby hat he gave her husband year before last. But when he clears the boundary of his county, when he bustles into an unfamiliar garage ten miles away and

With a flivver and some canvas anybody could go anywhere, and even take the family pets along. The auto tourist's uniform: khaki breeches and shirt.

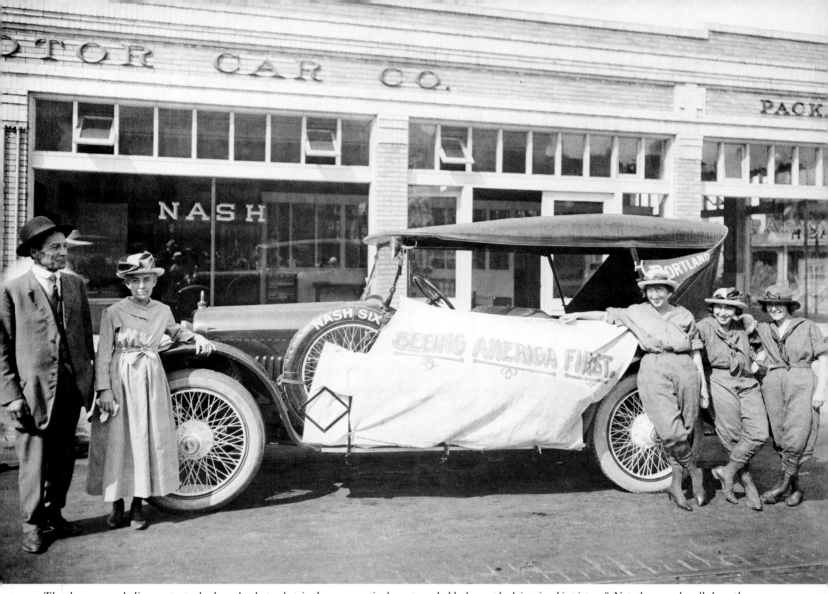

The three young ladies are properly dressed—but what is the conservatively costumed elderly couple doing in this picture? Note luggage bundled on the left-hand running board; early autos had no trunk and the roof wouldn't support a luggage rack. En route, tourists used the right-hand doors only.

snaps at the foreman that he wants his differential filled with grease, and he wants it quick, he discovers that news doesn't travel so fast as people say it does—this scoundrel hasn't yet heard the news about Mr. Average Citizen's importance. And after five days out, when the grease has mined into the backs of his hands and his last clean shirt isn't clean, he will be meek when the hoboes along the road grunt at him: "Hey, Billy, gimme a match! Where'd yuh steal de road louse?"

At first he won't like it. He will take hours and hours in telling his wife—sitting beside him and unable to escape without kicking off the switch and crawling out over six suitcases on the running board—that, outside of their hometown, people have no friendliness. But after ten days he will revel in being part of the land, of long roads and quiet fields and sloping lovely hills and placid people content to live alone. He will stop worrying about the indubitable ways in which his assistant can ruin his business. He will recover from his ancient irritation about his neighbor's early rising guinea hens. He may even partially forget that a man of his dignity

has to act to his own small universe as the representative and image of the Almighty. And when he comes back all men will wonder at his jolly, whimsical modesty—for minutes and minutes they will.

I had a new car once and a new overcoat, and by request I wasn't wearing the comfortable shoes, but the good-looking ones. I was driving from New York to Chicago with a personage. He was a war correspondent just back from Russia. He had once made love to an Italian princess and he possesses—almost free of debt—an acre of ground near New York, which is the same as owning all of Siberia. We gave ourselves a rating of about ninety h. p. and we looked with pity on all cars which were muddy. Of course we had been through a little mud ourselves and since noon we had washed our hands only when filling the radiator—a heathen custom which consists in spilling half of a can of water on your trousers and the other half on the hood. But nobody could notice those blots on us—no, not possibly.

We came with languid distinction into a small hotel in

The West of Yesterday

Famed illustrator N. C. Wyeth painted this Western scene. The car is a 1915 model.

Ohio. The war correspondent condescended to the landlady in his best Yale and Piccadilly voice: "May we have dinner here?"

She looked us all over. I was prepared to tell her, when she asked, that the new overcoat hadn't really cost a hundred. She smiled gently. She piped: "You boys driving cars through from the factory, or are you private chauffeurs?"

We ate dinner—which wasn't dinner, but supper—with reticence, and we addressed the waitress in tones of humility, and when she snapped at the war correspondent "Tea or coffee, Joe?" he stretched out his paws and purred. We went out and looked, not at the newness and streamlineness of the car but at the mud that clotted the wheels and the general sloppiness of the suitcases in

the back; and our hearts were God's little gardens and we completely ceased thinking that we were persons of interest.

And we remained so, because on the next day a peculiarly smeary and recently immigrated Greek bootblack demanded of us, "You fellow drive a truck t'rough?" We knew he was flattering us. He really thought that we were driving a garbage wagon.

On another trip my wife and I were heading westward through a sagebrush desert. As it was after six we were discussing the one subject of real importance to the universe—would we get a decent dinner, and a mattress which wasn't a clay model of the Rocky Mountains, scale one inch to the mile? We stopped a flivver to ask about the hotels ahead.

The West of Today

The faithful flivver Sinclair Lewis drove west was a Ford of about the same vintage.

It was the dirtiest flivver we had yet seen. The hood was so thick with just-caked-grease that it seemed to be cased in gray alpaca. The casings were channeled to the bone. On the running board rode a trunk covered with the flowered-and-stippled tin which, in 1870, was regarded as especially suited to travel and in the tonneau was a rusty stove with frayed gunny sacking thrown over it. The man wore a blue denim shirt, a black felt hat and either he was unable to grow a beard or he had not shaved since starting from Vladivostok. His wife had a visored-and-puckered motor bonnet with eruptions of green veiling.

We stopped and spoke to them gently. We probably had a lot of satisfaction out of being superior and kindly. The vicar's wife permanently relieving poverty by distributing a potato every Whitsuntide had nothing on us for sweetness to the worthy poor.

It is true that we were driving a flivver ourselves that trip. But you know how it is. Your flivver is different from all other flivvers. It is smarter and racier and sportier and a lot more powerful. The only reason you have so much difficulty in picking it out from the others at the parking space is because you have dust in your eyes.

So from our sultan of the sand we pleasantly inquired: "What kind of hotel is there in the next town?"

The man smiled with the good fellowship of the road and shouted: "Pretty good place." His wife whispered something to him. He stopped. He glanced us over. He scratched his head and went on doubtfully: "I don't know as you'll want to stay there. It's expensive."

"How expensive?"

Pityingly—"They want seventy-five cents a night for a room for two!"

As we drove on——

Oh, Burns wouldn't have asked for that giftie of seeing ourselves as others see us if he had ever taken a long motor run. It's valuable for the soul, but it's extremely injurious to the faculty for talking haughtily to office boys and roaring at old bookkeepers. Especially hard on this form of self-ecstasy is contact with strange garage men along the way.

Garage men are—to one who has just taken a tour—not merely topics of discussion, like matrimony or Lloyd George. They are principles of ethics, like prohibition or the rise in copper.

I have asserted that practically any driver can stand a four-thousand-mile trip. But I must admit that the auto hobo should be prepared for calamities:

Every third man of whom you ask a direction will say: "Well, I'm a stranger here myself."

The right rear spring will break just after nightfall, when you leave the macadam and hit ten miles of what the man in the last town called "A short stretch of dirt road—might be just a leetle muddy now."

Every day at ten and eleven-thirty A. M., two-sixteen, five-twenty and eleven-fifty-six P. M. you will remember that you mustn't forget to replace the grease cup that has jarred off—and when you get back home it will still be missing.

There is no use of looking to see if the taillight bulb is burned out. It is.

There is always a better road than the one on the map and if you follow the farmer's advice and take it you will always get lost.

Your partner doesn't want to hear the detailed story of your breakdown—he's waiting to tell you his.

And last and more funereally certain, the garage man will act almost as though he thought you were a fool. There is an interesting psychological reason for that. He does think so.

You will see a great deal of garage men, no matter how much your wife thinks you know. Of course you may have luck—I know an amateur who drove seventeen hundred miles over corduroy and cut-over roads north and west of Lake Superior without a single puncture, without once having to look at his motor. But again—you may be certain of one axiom of repairs: There's always something new that can happen to a car. Whenever you wait in suspense for something you will probably go on for a thousand miles untouched; and whenever you feel that nothing can happen the bearings are just then burning out.

There wasn't a word for it in English, so the French "garage" was borrowed as a name for the place where we kept our cars or had them repaired. For a long time pronunciation varied; some said "GARE-ridge" while others said "gar-RARGE."

Slow—Sound Horn

By Courtney Ryley Cooper, 1922

THE DOCTOR in my little Rocky Mountain town asked me to write this story—as a favor to him and to other doctors who live in the hills and who, in the love of Nature, dislike to see the landscape muddled up with the wrecks of humans and automobiles, to say nothing of what it may do for those humans themselves who start out on a vacation with a glorious prospect—and end in a hospital.

"It's not that I object to the work," he told me, "even though it is a bit trying to hurry thirty miles or so up into the higher hills and try to load someone with a broken hip into an automobile and bring him to town, only to find that the fracture is such that it requires an X

ray before setting, thus necessitating a further trip of forty miles to a city and its well-equipped hospitals. It's just that there's no sense in it—and any doctor who's really a true member of his profession believes far more in prevention than in cure."

Hence this little effusion on how to avoid being killed while on your vacation! And in spite of the jocularity of it all, I happen to live in a country where persons seem to insist on needlessly killing themselves during their annual rest period; which, after all, is hardly the way to spend a vacation. It ruins not only their outing but that of everyone else; therefore these few scattered facts about a country which is a foreign land to the majority of the population of the United States, but a desired land, nevertheless, especially at vacation time—the mountains. . . .

What may seem strange to the uninitiated, and not at all strange to those who know the hills and who see the occupants of every fourth or fifth car literally shaking dice with death, is the fact that most of these accidents happen when the car is either stopped or going down-hill!

Naturally there is a logical explanation. The usual man, when he stops on a hill in town or in the country, sets his emergency brake; and then, if this does not hold tightly enough, reinforces this by throwing the car into

low gear or reverse, thus making the engine accomplish what the brake bands do not. On the ordinary grade, when the time comes to start again, the pull of the hill is so slight that if the emergency allows movement at all it is so slow as to be almost imperceptible. But on a mountain grade conditions are different. One can't throw the car out of gear and then step on the starter, trusting the brakes to hold until the engine starts. The pull of gravity is so strong that the minute that extra bindage is released the car starts downhill, and with speed! The result is that the driver, frightened by the strange actions of his car, loses his head for an instant—and that instant is enough. Mountain roads are narrow. They also are crooked. Upon the usual pass road a fifty-foot progress or regress in a straight line inevitably brings a car either to the edge of a precipice or into the stone wall of the mountain itself. There's a crash either way.

Yet it all is easily avoided—second nature, in fact, to mountaineers. The man who drives mountain roads merely turns off the ignition, and allows his car to stop in gear, at the extreme edge of the road if he is alone, or at any place he cares to if he is accompanied. Then the first action upon leaving the car is to place a good-sized chuck rock under a hind wheel. After which he can even release the brakes if he cares to—the rock does the braking for him. When he starts, if alone, he has come from a far side of the road, where the chuck rock will not bother the next motorist, because it is out of the line of travel. If he is accompanied his companion stands at the rear of the car and throws the chuck from the highway, and then catches up with the slow-moving machine and hops in. Very simple to the mountain driver. A bit inconvenient, perhaps, to the man accustomed to the cities or to the smooth white roads of the East. . . .

There are curves, curves, curves, and constant meetings with machines that slink around them as though they had been lying in wait to force a victim off the road. There are meetings in which cars are forced to back, sometimes as much as a hundred feet or so, to a turnout, and backing on a grade is not an easy task. So withal it begins to eat in, deeper, deeper—until at last the driver loses his control and becomes panicky. The machine is constantly all but getting away from him, even if he runs on compression; in his nervousness he forgets that he is putting his foot on the gas lever and shoving up the speed. In a case like this there is only one remedy, but a sure one—stop the machine, get out, find the sturdiest of one of the innumerable dead trees that are always a part of the surroundings of a mountain pass. Drag it to the road and tie it on behind your machine. The extra weight of that drag will slow up the machine to such an extent that you move with snail-like progress and, during that lull, regain your composure.

But suppose you haven't a stout rope? Well—if you haven't, or if you don't know how to examine your engine, your brakes, your oil and cooling system; if you don't carry a container of oil and gas, a collapsible bucket for obtaining water from near-by brooks, a good set of tools, a few parts that may be substituted for those in most danger of breaking, a spade, a good extra tire, and a head that can assimilate simple rules and follow them——

Don't drive in the mountains!

The pleasures rather than the perils of mountain driving are suggested here; the cars are 1928 Cadillacs. By 1928 most buyers wanted closed cars and the open auto was beginning to be a status symbol. One assumed the owner also had a snug sedan for winter driving.

Perhaps the most vulnerable of the automobile's parts, tires occupied much of the motorist's attention. On this page, a 1923 advertisement for the B. F. Goodrich Rubber Company. Opposite, a 1922 Post *cover.*

BEST IN T   LONG RUN

GOODRICH SILVERTOWN CORD

The World Isn't Finished

By Charles F. "Boss" Kettering, Vice President of General Motors in Charge of Research, 1932

A MAN SAID TO ME THE OTHER DAY, "I don't see what you can do to improve the automobile. It looks like perfection to me." I said, "I hope it isn't, because my job is gone if it is." And that's a fact. Most of our jobs would be gone if the products of the industries in which we are engaged should be adjudged perfect. Because then it would be a question of employing just enough men to produce the perfect thing, and not more than 30 percent of us would have employment.

We in the automobile business bring out early models on the theory that business and social conditions progress as producers hit a constant rate of improvement. We believe that for the

next ten or twenty years at least we can bring to you an improved and a better automobile. I think I can illustrate the basis for my belief by considering the three basic materials with which we work—rubber, petroleum and steel.

I always admired the man Dunlop, because I think that anybody that had the nerve to propose a rubber tire to run on the ground when everybody knew that steel was the only thing that would do, must have been a man of distinct nerve and bravery. He planted the idea, and the simple rubber tube that he made progressed through various stages of evolution, until, a half dozen years or so ago, the industry turned out the balloon tire. Mileages went from three and four thousand miles up to fifteen and twenty thousand. We began to experience a new ease in riding and a new safety in driving.

Thus, to the rubber people we owe a great debt. Yet, I don't think their job is finished. In this line alone, we can expect tremendous improvement, even revolutionary developments.

COLES PHILLIPS

17 Billion Gallons of Gas

By Samuel G. Blythe, 1930

THE FIRST GASOLINE I EVER SAW in quantity was at an Eastern refinery somewhat more than forty years ago. It was a waste product, thrown away. It had no value and no uses. Kerosene was what the refiners were after in those days. Gasoline, produced by the lighter vapors rising during the processes of refining crude petroleum, was a nuisance, an outlaw. It was explosive and dangerous. It annoyed the refiners exceedingly. They cursed it with vehemence, and oil men are vehement cursers. It interfered with the orderly conduct of the business of getting kerosene for the lamps of the world. The miserable stuff was dumped on the ground or burned. There was nothing else to do with it. I reckon that 45.6 percent of all the profanity around the refineries of those days had its genesis in this gosh-durned gasoline that gummed things up by being a constant source of danger in the way of fire and explosive slaughter, and persisted in appearing every time they set out to make a mess of good, marketable kerosene.

Then, in 1892, there appeared a vehicle for which the power of progress was furnished by an engine that utilized gasoline as the impelling fuel. This pariah of the oil trade actually stepped in and motivated a cumbersome carriage at a speed of, say, twenty miles an hour without the aid of horses, steam or any other object or element whatsoever. Incredible, but true.

The hated outlaw, gasoline, turned respectable at that moment and demanded an honest place in the commodity family of the world.

By 1900 there were 8,000 registered automobiles in this country that moved about by virtue of the powers concealed within the former outcast, gasoline. Instead of throwing gasoline away, the refiners sold 260,000,000 gallons of it that year.

Sold it, you understand. Got real money for the stuff they formerly discarded—this gasoline that was such a condemned nuisance when it gummed up kerosene production by persisting to rise in the refinery stills, along with naphtha, before the valued kerosene made any movement toward getting into the game. Well, what do you think of that? What would you have thought of it if you had been the refiners and had sold, for cash or its equivalent, 260,000,000 gallons of stuff that, only a few years before, wasn't worth a nickel an oceanful?

Not being in business for any other purpose than to make money, you know what the refiners thought. They thought there might be value in this pediculous gasoline after all, and they began to conserve it instead of cussing it. They felt that something might be coming—which showed a commendable intuition on their part. Something was coming, and it came with a sweep of demand that was the foundation of the enormous oil business of the present day.

In 1922 motorists paid about 26 cents a gallon—except where there was a "gas war" to bring the price down to something more reasonable.

D. B.

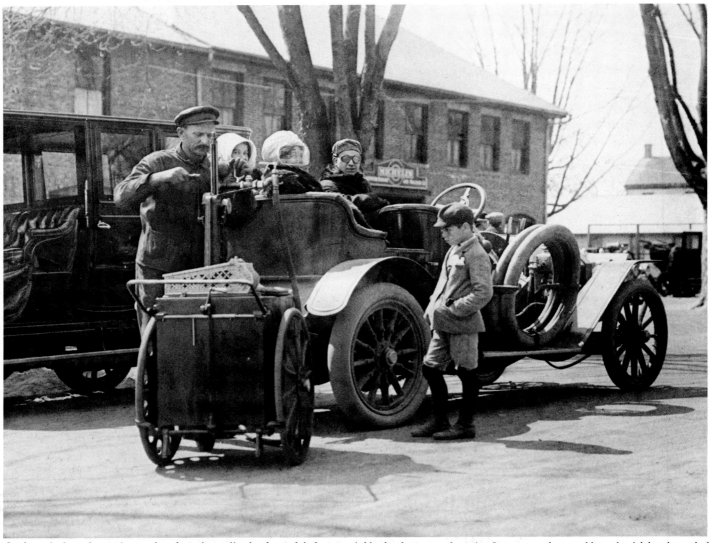

In the early days of motoring one bought one's gasoline by the canful, from a neighborhood grocer or druggist. Later came the portable tank with hand-cranked pump shown above and, at the left of the shed, below. Some thought the shortened word "gas" vulgar; "like saying 'butt' for butter," remarks a Mary Roberts Rinehart character in a 1912 Post *story.*

I do not know how many more cars than the 8,000 gasoline-impelled cars of 1900 there were in 1901, but I do know that in this year of 1930 there are 26,500,000 of them in the United States and about 9,000,000 more in the rest of the world, of which a great proportion were made in this country. Also, I know that the gasoline engines of this country will use this year 17,000,000,000 gallons of gasoline. . . .

Back in the early '90s when E. K. Duryea and other pioneers were demonstrating that a horseless carriage or a benzine buggy was a feasible mode of transportation, these men and the other hardy adventurers who had faith and bought cars got their gasoline where they could—mostly from the grocer, who grudgingly put in the dangerous stuff as a sideline and stored it in and vended it from tin cans. The engines were embryonic in those days compared to the present engines in use, and the cars were clumsy. The motorist who went out for a drive was not sure whether he could accomplish five miles or twenty-five before some gadget slipped, or something went wrong with the combustion, or a tire blew out, or the durned thing just refused to go.

So recently as 1897, after President McKinley was inaugurated and had been in office a few weeks, J. Addison Porter, the secretary to the President, invited the Washington correspondents over to the White House one morning to report fully the epochal event of the first horseless carriage to enter the White House grounds accomplishing that marvelous feat. At the appointed time, or thereabouts, the miracle was performed. Colonel Pope, one of the great pioneers in the automobile industry, drove majestically up in what, if my memory serves, was a Pope-Toledo car, and circled the driveway several times, much to the gratification of the President and many other distinguished personages who stood on the portico, and greatly to the honor and increment of the American spirit of invention. And all the newspapers of the day that had Washington correspondents printed first-page stories about it all. . . .

A variant of the cutthroat competition that has silvered the hair of the oil marketing man is the price wars. These occur here and there, and now and then, and are particularly virulent on the Pacific Coast, where a large amount of the country's gasoline is made. Things will be going quietly out there, with gasoline at its accustomed prices all along the Coast and some outlaw and bootleg stations cutting the price a bit, when suddenly, without warning to the consumers, but, possibly, with inside information to the producers, some company will cut the price per retail gallon three cents, five cents, or whatever sum is determined upon.

The wholesalers must have a fine intelligence system, for instantly all of them are apprised of this cut, and almost instantly they meet the cut. After that a very fair imitation of chaos in a big business prevails, for further cuts are made and the consumer gaily gets the better of it. For once the consumer has a break. In the latest price war on the Coast, which happened in midsummer, gasoline was sold for as little as three cents a gallon in some parts of California. Inasmuch as the California state tax on gasoline is three cents, which the producers collect, the wholesalers who were selling to the three-cent stations got exactly nothing at all for their gas. Oh, happy day for the motorists!

The price wars do not last long, but they are very nourishing to the consumers while they do last.

By 1924 the service station had evolved. The gas pumps were permanently attached to underground tanks but they still had to be cranked by hand.

The best known of all auto slogans, "Ask the man who owns one," appeared with this 1936 advertisement and all others for the Packard, a fine automobile manufactured in Warren, Ohio, 1900-1902, and in Detroit, 1902-1954. On the opposite page, a 1933 Cadillac.

When a Nation Sits on a Throne

Automobile Advertisement, 1931

THIS NEW ERA of widespread personal power is filling so strange a place in history that even those of us who are thinking about it are baffled most of the time.

We buy an automobile, for example, and plump ourselves down into its soft seats, never realizing that the untold millions of people who have swept through history have lived and died without even the vainest dream of the power that comes to us with the simple turning of a switch and the pressure of a toe.

We are like a nation of kings, each of us on his own throne, behind the wheel of his own power.

If you want to get a thrill which will stay with you for the rest of your life, stop your car sometime when you are in some far distant land, call one of the peasants in from the field, put him, barefooted, at the wheel, and spend an hour in teaching him to drive. Gradually, as the fear goes out of him and this thing of life comes under his control, you will see his gnarled hands grip the wheel, you'll see his shoulders straighten and a look of awe come into his face that you will never forget.

And you will suddenly realize that what you are looking at is the thing that mankind has been striving for through all the centuries—that longing for personal power that has suddenly been fulfilled.

We say quite casually to a friend, "I've just bought a new car." And we get in and drive off without ever a thought of what it means in the history of the world. We swing down the boulevard with a sense of equality and of personal power such as the world in its past has only dreamed of in its wildest dreams.

We have a carriage of wood and steel and beauty beside which any of the old coaches of state seem crude and cumbersome. We have a motor the feel of which transcends any previous sense of power mankind has ever known. And a speed which in any of the old mythologies would have given us the quality of gods.

And yet, because we live in this strange era, because ours is a part of this new equality of power, because nothing like us has ever happened before, we sum it all up in the casual remark, "I've just bought a new car."

I Dream Automobiles

by Harley J. Earl, Chief of
General Motors' Styling Section, 1954

I HAVE IN MY OFFICE a scale model of the first sedan I ever designed for the company, a 1927 LaSalle V-8. I have a great affection for the old crock, but I must admit it is slab-sided, top-heavy and stiff-shouldered. At the same time there is something on it that explains very simply what I have been trying to do and hope I have done in the last twenty-eight years.

On the line we now call the beltline, running around the body just below the windows, there is a decorative strip something like half a figure 8 fastened to the body. This strip was placed there to eat up the overpowering vertical expanse of that tall car. It was an effort to make the car look longer and lower.

There you have it. My primary purpose for twenty-eight years has been to lengthen and lower the American automobile, at times in reality and always at least in appearance. Why? Because my sense of proportion tells me that oblongs are more attractive than squares, just as a ranch house is more attractive than a square, three-story, flat-roofed house or a greyhound is more graceful than an English bulldog. Happily, the car-buying public and I consistently agree on this. . . .

There is no doubt that car buyers have approved this basic change in the automobile's conformation, but while we are very careful indeed to guard the passenger's comfort during any process of styling change, there are always some indignant critics. The most amusing brickbats I get are occasional letters accusing me of being a shrimp and wanting to squash passengers down to the ground to suit my own anatomy. This happens only in letters. It would be silly for anyone to say it to my face, as I am six feet four inches tall and weigh over 200.

Of course, we realize very well that Americans are touchy about their automobiles. Their cars are usually treasured possessions and they definitely want to have a warm, friendly feeling about them and to feel thoroughly at home in them. We also know that to build this relationship between car and owner into the automobile itself is an elusive task. . . .

The question of chrome brightwork always comes up in automobile discussions. Now, I am not particularly committed to chrome; it fact, I think it would be interesting if the brass industry would provide us with some warm-colored brass that wouldn't have to be polished. Maybe it will someday. But when chrome arrived as a decorative trim for the industry, it was imperative that I find out how people really felt about it. Consequently I had to turn ten of my top staff into temporary private eyes. They were dispatched to key cities to pose as newspaper reporters among used-car lots and new-car salesrooms, where the car buyer seriously registers his reactions by selecting cars. They asked hundreds of questions about customer response to or rejection of chrome trim. The conclusions were in favor of chrome, more so on used-car lots, slightly less in new-car salesrooms. This difference may be accounted for in the fact that used-car buyers average slightly under thirty years of age, whereas new-car buyers average three and one-half years older.

Certain evolutions in design have always struck me as inevitable. Long ago I was convinced that the elongation of both front and back fenders would eventually merge them to produce a single flowing sideline from front to back. I was equally sure this front-to-back body line would be rounded vertically so that the beltline would present a continuous highlight, a very important

visual factor. On our handmade initial models we test the presence of this highlight by playing strong lights on the body from every direction. And even in 1928 I felt strongly that windshields would slant farther and farther, and I hoped that someday we would be able to move the corner pillars out of the way to provide really sweeping vision. That day has arrived, and our 1954 cars carry the panoramic windshield that wraps around the corners to pillars that have been offset from the straight vertical. . . .

There is a touch of Oldfield and De Palma in most Americans, and frankly I wonder sometimes if there isn't a trace of the old Santa Monica race track in every car I've ever designed. This might be a good time to confess, too, that I have been deeply affected by airplanes. I was so excited by the P-38 Lockheed Lightning when I first saw it that I contrived a viewing for members of my staff.

We had to stand thirty feet away from it because it was still in security, but even at that distance we could soak up the lines of its twin booms and twin tails.

Wartime advertising served to keep auto-makers' names before the public and to whet the appetite for things to come in peacetime. This 1944 ad shows the twin-fuselage P-38 fighter plane that inspired the soaring tailfins of the 1959 Cadillac below.

That viewing, after the war ended, blossomed out in the Cadillac fishtail fenders which subsequently spread through our cars and over much of the industry as well. The so-called fishtail descendant of the P-38 on the Cadillac started slowly because it was a fairly sharp departure. But it caught on widely after that because ultimately Cadillac owners realized that it gave them an extra receipt for their money in the form of a visible prestige marking for an expensive car.

A further point about the fishtail was that it helped give some graceful bulk to the automobile, and I have felt for a long time that Americans like a good-sized automobile as long as it is nicely proportioned and has a dynamic, go-ahead look. Conversely, I have never seen any evidence that needle-front or thin models were to the American taste. I think the history of front grilles bears me out on this. Aside from being a logical help to the engineers in placing the radiator at an efficient location, the front grille has always given American cars a comfortably blunt, leonine front look. This is good, as long as the car as a whole is poised right. There was a time when automobiles tilted down in front as if they intended to dig for woodchucks. Subsequently they went tail-heavy and appeared to be sitting up and begging. Now I think we have them in exactly the right attitude of level alertness, like an airplane at take-off. . . .

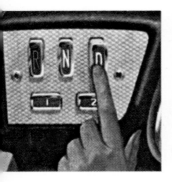

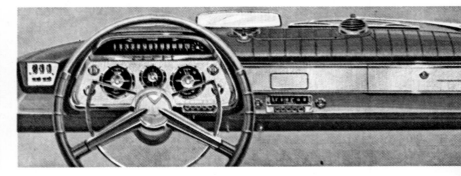

That's the way it goes in designing. Most of our thousands of hours of work every year are small refinements and revisions to improve the comfort, utility and appearance of our automobiles. But we also need explosive bursts of spanking-new themes, and somehow we get them. I have enjoyed every minute of both kinds of this labor for twenty-eight years, and just a few months ago I was reminded again of the long way automobile design has come and the fact that there is no end to it. I was observing the Chevrolet Nomad station wagon in the 1954 Motorama, and it was clear that my long-time effort to lower American automobiles had indeed succeeded. I was looking right across the top of the Nomad's roof. And there was visible evidence that every accomplishment can raise a new problem. To an average man, the Nomad's roof was now visible as a part of the car's conformation. So, for perhaps the first time in automobile history, we had had to give this unbroken roof expanse a decorative treatment. We grooved it. I hope designing is always like that.

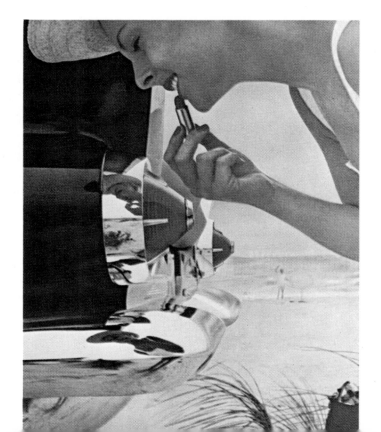

High tide for chrome trim, the two- and three-color paint job, the fishtail fin. Opposite page: the 1960 Cadillac and the 1959 Dodge, with detail of the Dodge's push-button shift, headlamps and dashboard. On this page: the 1960 Buick, the 1959 Chevrolet (going, not coming), and a young lady demonstrating the usefulness of shiny trim. Physicians and safety engineers took a dim view of these cars because of sharp-pointed protuberances which could impale the unwary pedestrian.

Men, Women and Motors

Some of the most unforgettable characters in American fiction are noble horses, lovable dogs—and capricious automobiles. On the following pages are selections from the work of four important writers who grew up with cars and wrote about them with affection and humor. Here, a 1929 Whippet (manufactured 1926-1931 by Willys-Overland) in a setting right for F. Scott Fitzgerald.

Hell Creek Crossing

By William Faulkner

The year is 1905, the locale is Faulkner country—rural Mississippi. The narrator in this excerpt from The Reivers *is an 11-year-old boy whose parents and grandparents have been called away to a relative's funeral, leaving behind the grandfather's 1904-model automobile. Temptation is too much for the boy and two men who work for his family, the huge part-Chickasaw Boon Hogganbeck and Ned, an elderly ex-slave. The three set off toward Memphis, over roads that were not yet ready for the automobile age. A woman along the route reports they are "the thirteenth automobile to pass there in the last two years, five of them in the last forty days; she had already lost two hens and would probably have to begin keeping everything penned up, even the hounds."*

THE SUN WAS JUST RISING as we crossed the iron bridge over the river into foreign country, another county; by night it would even be another state, and Memphis.

"Providing we get through Hell Creek," Boon said.

"Maybe if you'd just stop talking about it," I said.

"Sure," Boon said, "Hell Creek bottom don't care whether you talk about it or not. It don't have to give a durn. You'll see." Then he said, "Well, there it is." It was only a little after ten; we had made excellent time following the ridges, the roads dry and dusty between the sprouting fields, the land vacant and peaceful with Sunday, the people already in their Sunday clothes idle on the front galleries, the children and dogs already running toward the fence or road to watch us pass; then in the surreys and buggies and wagons and on horse and muleback, anywhere from one to three on the horse but not on the mule (A little after nine we had passed another automobile, Boon said it was a Ford; he had an eye for automobiles like Miss Ballenbaugh's.) on the way to the small white church in the spring groves.

A wide valley lay before us, the road descending from the plateau toward a band of willow and cypress which marked the creek. It didn't look very bad to me, nowhere near as wide as the river bottom we had already crossed, and we could even see the dusty gash of the road mounting to the opposite plateau beyond it.

A 1905 Saturday Evening Post *cover shows a car typical of the period.*

"City or country, hill or level—all roads are alike," says advertising for this 1906 Oldsmobile Gentleman's Roadster. Price: $2,250.

But Boon had already started to curse, driving even faster down the hill almost as if he were eager, anxious to reach and join battle with it, as if it were something sentient, not merely inimical but unredeemable, like a human enemy, another man. "Look at it," he said. "Innocent as a new-laid egg. You can even see the road beyond it like it was laughing at us, like it was saying, 'If you could just get here you could durn near see Memphis; except just see if you can get here.' "

"If it's all that bad, why don't we go around it?" Ned said. "That's what I would do if it was me setting there where you is."

"Because Hell Creek bottom ain't got no around," Boon said violently. "Go one way and you'd wind up in Alabama; go the other way and you'll fall off in the Missippi River."

"I seen the Missippi River at Memphis once," Ned said. "Now you mention it, I done already seen Memphis too. But I ain't never seen Alabama. Maybe I'd like a trip there."

"You ain't never visited Hell Creek bottom before neither," Boon said. "Providing what you hid under that tarpollyon for yesterday is education. Why do you reckon the only two automobiles we have seen between now and Jefferson was this one and that Ford? Because there ain't no other automobiles in Missippi below Hell Creek, that's why."

"Miss Ballenbaugh counted thirteen passed her house in the last two years," I said.

"Two of them was this one," Boon said. "And even them other eleven she never counted crossing Hell Creek, did she?"

"Maybe it depends on who's doing the driving," Ned said. "Hee hee hee."

Boon stopped the car quickly. He turned his head. "All right. Jump out. You want to visit Alabama. You done already made yourself fifteen minutes late running your mouth."

"Why you got to snatch a man up just for passing the day with you?" Ned said. But Boon wasn't listening to him. I don't think he was really speaking to Ned. He was already out of the car; he opened the toolbox grandfather had had made on the running board to hold the block and tackle and ax and spade and the lantern, taking everything out but the lantern and tumbling them into the back seat with Ned.

"So we won't waste any time," he said, speaking rapidly, but quite composed, calm, without hysteria or even urgency, closing the box and getting back under the wheel. "Let's hit it. What're we waiting for?"

Still it didn't look bad to me—just another country road crossing another swampy creek, the road no longer dry but not really wet yet, the holes and boggy places already filled for our convenience by previous pioneers with brush tops and limbs, and sections of it even corduroyed with poles laid crossways in the mud (oh yes, I realized suddenly that the road—for lack of any closer term—had stopped being not really wet yet too), so perhaps Boon himself was responsible; he himself had populated the stagnant cypress- and willow-arched mosquito-whined gloom with the wraiths of stuck automobiles and sweating and cursing people. Then I thought we had struck it, except for that fact that I not only couldn't see any rise of drier ground which would indicate we were reaching, approaching the other side of the swamp, I couldn't even see the creek itself ahead yet, let alone a bridge. Again the automobile lurched, canted and hung as it did yesterday at Hurricane Creek; again Boon was already removing his shoes and socks and rolling up his pants. "All right," he said to Ned over his shoulder, "get out."

"I don't know how," Ned said. "I ain't learned about automobiles yet. I'd be in your way. I'll set here with Lucius so you can have plenty of room."

"Hee hee hee," Boon said in savage and vicious mimicry. "You wanted a trip. Now you got one. Get out."

"I got my Sunday clothes on," Ned said, not moving.

"So have I," Boon said. "If I ain't scared of a pair of britches, you needn't be."

"You can talk," Ned said. "You got Mr. Maury. I has to work for my money. When my clothes gets ruint or wore out, I has to buy new ones myself."

"You never bought a garment of clothes or shoes or a hat neither in your life," Boon said. "You got one pigeon-tailed coat I know of that old Lucius McCaslin himself wore, let alone General Compson's and Major de Spain's and Boss's too. You can roll your britches up and take off your shoes or not—that's your business. But you're going to get out of this automobile."

"Let Lucius get out," Ned said. "He's younger than me and stouter too for his size."

"He's got to steer it," Boon said.

"I'll steer it, if that's all you needs," Ned said. "I been what you calls steering horses and mules and oxen all my life and I reckon gee and haw with that steering wheel ain't no different from gee and haw with a pair of lines or a goad." Then to me: "Jump out, boy, and help Mr. Boon. Better take your shoes and stockings——"

"Are you going to get out, or do I pick you up with one hand and snatch this automobile out from under you with the other?" Boon said. Ned moved then, fast enough when he finally accepted the fact that he had to, only grunting a little as he took off his shoes and rolled

Unfortunately, Americans were ready to take to the road in their new vehicles before America's roads were ready for them (1909).

Traveling by auto was an adventure, and the well-equipped motorist carried a folding Kodak for recording roadside triumphs and tragedies. (1907)

up his pants and removed his coat. When I looked back at Boon, he was already dragging two poles, sapling-sized tree trunks, out of the weeds and briers.

"Ain't you going to use the block and tackle yet?" I said.

"Hell no," Boon said. "When the time comes for that, you won't need to ask nobody's permission about it. You'll already know it." *So it's the bridge*, I thought. *Maybe there's not even a bridge at all and that's what's wrong.* And Boon read my mind there too. "Don't worry about the bridge. We ain't even come to the bridge yet."

I would learn what he meant by that too, but not now. Ned lowered one foot gingerly into the water. "This water got dirt in it," he said. "If there's one thing I hates, it's dirt betwixt my nekkid toes."

"That's because your circulation ain't warmed up yet," Boon said. "Take a holt of this pole. You said you

ain't acquainted with automobiles yet. That's one complaint you won't never have to make again for the rest of your life. All right"—to me—"ease her ahead now, and whenever she bites, keep her going." Which we did, Boon and Ned levering their poles forward under the back axle, pinching us forward for another lurch of two or three or sometimes five feet, until the car hung spinning again, the whirling back wheels coating them both from knee to crown as if they had been swung at with one of the spray nozzles which house painters use.

"See what I mean," Boon said, spitting, giving another terrific wrench and heave which sent us lurching forward, "about getting acquainted with automobiles? Exactly like horses and mules: Don't never stand behind one that's got one hind foot already lifted."

Then I saw the bridge. We had come up onto a patch of earth so (comparatively) dry that Boon and Ned,

No etiquette book would have approved the unconventional behavior of this madcap group, lost in the forest in their 1916 Overlands.

almost indistinguishable now with mud, had to trot with their poles and even then couldn't keep up, Boon hollering, panting, "Go on! Keep going!" until I saw the bridge a hundred yards ahead and then saw what was still between us and the bridge, and I knew what he meant. I stopped the car. The road (the passage, whatever you would call it now) in front of us had not altered so much as it had transmogrified, exchanged mediums, elements. It now resembled a big receptacle of milk-infused coffee from which protruded here and there a few forlorn, impotent, hopeless odds and ends of sticks and brush and logs and an occasional hump of actual earth which looked startlingly like it had been deliberately thrown up by a plow. Then I saw something else and understood what Boon had been telling me by indirection about Hell Creek bottom for over a year now, and what he had been reiterating with a kind of haunted, bemused obsession ever since we left Jefferson

yesterday. Standing hitched to a tree just off the road (canal) were two mules in plow gear—that is, in bridles and collars and hames, the trace chains looped over the hames and the plowlines coiled into neat hanks and hanging from the hames also; leaning against another tree nearby was a heavy double-winged plow—a middlebuster—caked (wings, shank and the beam itself) with more of the same mud which was rapidly encasing Boon and Ned, a doubletree, likewise mud-caked, leaning against the plow; and, in the immediate background, a new two-room paintless shotgun cabin on the gallery of which a man sat tilted in a splint chair, barefoot, his galluses down about his waist and his (likewise muddy) brogan shoes against the wall beside the chair. And I knew that this, and not Hurricane Creek, was where (Boon said) he and Mr. Wordwin had had to borrow the shovel last year, which (Boon said) Mr. Wordwin had forgot to return, and which (the

What joy, being young when the automobile was young! No earlier generation enjoyed such freedom to go and come sans servant or chaperone.

shovel) Mr. Wordwin might as well have forgot to borrow also for all the good it did them.

Ned had seen it too. He had already had one hard look at the mudhole. Now he looked at the already geared-up mules standing there swishing and slapping at mosquitoes while they waited for us. "Now, that's what I calls convenient," he said.

"Shut up," Boon said in a fierce murmur. "Not a word. Don't make a sound." He spoke in a tense, controlled fury, propping his muddy pole against the car and hauling out the block and tackle and the barbed wire and the ax and spade. He said "son of a bitch" three times. Then he said to me: "You too."

"Me?" I said.

"But look at them mules," Ned said. "He even got a log chain already hooked to that doubletree——"

"Didn't you hear me say shut up?" Boon said in that fierce, quite courteous murmur. "If I didn't speak plain enough, excuse me. What I'm trying to say is, shut up."

"Only, what in the world do he want with the middlebuster?" Ned said. "And it muddy clean up to the handles too. Like he been—you mean to say he gets in here with that team and works this place like a patch just to keep it boggy?"

Boon had the spade, ax and block and tackle all three in his hands. For a second I thought he would strike Ned with any or maybe all three of them.

I said quickly: "What do you want me——"

"Yes," Boon said. "It will take all of us. I—me and Mr. Wordwin had a little trouble with him here last year; we got to get through this time."

"How much did you have to pay him last year to get drug out?" Ned said.

"Two dollars," Boon said. "So you better take off your whole pants. Take off your shirt too; it'll be all right here."

"There's exhilaration in a dash into the real country through the crisp autumn air, with perhaps a mountain stream to ford at full speed" (1911).

"Two dollars?" Ned said. "This sho beats cotton. He can farm right here setting in the shade without even moving. What I wants boss to get me is a well-traveled mudhole."

"Fine," Boon said. "You can learn how on this one." He gave Ned the block and tackle and the piece of barbed wire. "Take it yonder to that willow, the big one, and get a good holt with it." Ned payed out the rope and carried the head block to the tree. I took off my pants and shoes and stepped down into the mud. It felt good, cool. Maybe it felt that way to Boon too. Or maybe his—Ned's too—was just release, freedom from having to waste any time now trying not to get muddy. Anyway, from now on he simply ignored the mud, squatting in it, saying son of a bitch quietly and steadily while he fumbled the other piece of barbed wire into a loop on the front of the car to hook the block in. "Here," he told me, "you be dragging up some of that brush over yonder"—reading my mind again too—"I don't know

where it came from neither. Maybe he stacks it up there himself to keep handy for folks so they can find out good how bad they owe him two dollars."

So I dragged up the brush—branches, tops—into the mud in front of the car, while Boon and Ned took up the slack in the tackle and got ready, Ned and I on the take-up rope of the tackle, Boon at the back of the car with his prize pole again. "You got the easy job," he told us. "All you got to do is grab and hold when I heave. All right," he said, "let's go."

There was something dreamlike about it. Not nightmarish, just dreamlike—the peaceful, quiet, remote, sylvan, almost primeval setting of ooze and slime and jungle growth and heat in which the very mules themselves, peacefully swishing and stamping at the teeming, infinitesimal, invisible myriad life which was the actual air we moved and breathed in, were not only unalien but in fact curiously appropriate, being themselves biological dead ends and hence already obsolete before they were born; the automobile: the expensive useless mechanical toy rated in power and strength by the dozens of horses, yet held helpless and impotent in the almost infantile clutch of a few inches of the temporary confederation of two mild and pacific elements—earth and water—which the frailest integers and units of motion as produced by the ancient unmechanical methods had coped with for countless generations without really having noticed it; the three of us, three forked identical and now unrecognizable mud-colored creatures engaged in a life-and-death struggle with it, the progress—if any—of which had to be computed in dreadful and glacierlike inches. And all the while the man sat in his tilted chair on the gallery watching us while Ned and I strained for every inch we could get on the rope, which by now was too slippery with mud to grip with the hands; and at the rear of the car Boon strove like a demon, titanic, ramming his pole beneath the automobile and lifting and heaving it forward; at one time he dropped, flung away the pole and,

stooping, grasped the car with his hands and actually ran it forward for a foot or two as though it were a wheelbarrow. No man could stand it. No man should ever have to. I said so at last. I stopped pulling; I said, panted: "No, we can't do it. We just can't."

And Boon, in an expiring voice as faint and gentle as the whisper of love: "Then get out of the way or I'll run it over you."

"No," I said. I stumbled, slipping and plunging, back to him. "No," I said. "You'll kill yourself."

"I ain't tired," Boon said in that light dry voice. "I'm just getting started good. But you and Ned can take a rest. While you're getting your breath, suppose you drag up some more of that brush——"

"No," I said, "no! Here he comes! Do you want him to see it?" Because we could see him as well as hear—the suck and plop of the mules' feet as they picked their delicate way along the edge of the mudhole, the almost musical jangle of the looped chains, the man riding one and leading the other, his shoes tied together by the laces looped over one of the hames, the doubletree balanced in front of him as the old buffalo hunters in the

In advertisements the cars sailed on through mud and water. In real life this happened, and there was nothing to do but send for help.

pictures carried their guns, a gaunt man, older than we—I, anyway—had assumed.

"Morning, boys," he said. "Looks like you're about ready for me now. Howdy, Jefferson," he said to Boon. "Looks like you did get through last summer after all."

"Looks like it," Boon said. He had changed, instantaneous and complete, like a turned page: the poker player who has just seen the second deuce fall to a hand across the table. "We might 'a' got through this time too if you folks didn't raise such heavy mud up here."

"Don't hold that against us," the man said. "Mud's one of our best crops up thisaway."

"At two dollars a mudhole, it ought to be your best," Ned said. The man blinked at Ned a moment.

"I don't know but what you're right," he said. "Here. You take this doubletree; you look like a boy that knows which end of a mule to hook to."

"Get down and do it yourself," Boon said. "Why else are we paying you two dollars to be the hired expert? You done it last year."

"That was last year," the man said. "Dabbling around in this water hooking log chains to them things undermined my system to where I come down with rheumatism if I so much as spit on myself." So he didn't stir. He just brought the mules up and turned them side by side while Boon and Ned hooked the trace chains to the singletrees, and then Boon squatted in the mud to make the log chain fast to the car.

"What do you want me to hook it to?" he said.

"I don't care myself," the man said. "Hook up to any part of it you want out of this mudhole. If you want all of it to come out at the same time, I'd say hook to the axle. But first I'd put all them spades and ropes back in the automobile. You won't need them no more, at least here." So Ned and I did that, and Boon hooked up, and

we all three stood clear and watched. He was an expert, of course, but by now the mules were experts, too, breaking the automobile free of the mud, keeping the strain balanced on the doubletree as delicately as wire walkers, getting the automobile into motion and keeping it there with no more guidance than a word now and then from the man who rode the near mule and an occasional touch from the peeled switch he carried; on to where the ground was more earth than water.

"All right, Ned," Boon said. "Unhook him."

"Not yet," the man said. "There's another hole just this side of the bridge that I'm throwing in free. You ain't been acquainted here for a year now." He said to Ned: "What we call the reserve patch up thisaway."

"You means the Christmas middle," Ned said.

"Maybe I do," the man said. "What is it?"

Ned told him: "It's how we done at McCaslin back before the Surrender when old L.Q.C. was alive, and how the Edmonds boys still does. Every spring a middle is streaked off in the best ground on the place, and every stalk of cotton betwixt that middle and the edge of the field belongs to the Christmas fund, not for the boss but for every McCaslin nigger to have a Christmas share of it. That's what a Christmas middle is. Like you mud-farming folks up here never heard of it."

The man looked at Ned awhile. After a while Ned said, "Hee hee hee."

"That's better," the man said. "I thought for a minute me and you was about to misunderstand one another." He said to Boon: "Maybe somebody better guide it."

"Yes," Boon said. "All right," he told me. So I got under the wheel, mud and all. But we didn't move yet. The man said, "I forgot to mention it, so maybe I better. Prices have doubled around here since last year."

"Why?" Boon said. "It's the same car, the same

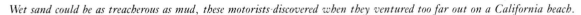

Wet sand could be as treacherous as mud, these motorists discovered when they ventured too far out on a California beach.

The mule has the last laugh, but if the farmer isn't smiling it is because he is too polite. The motorcar provided him with a new source of income.

mudhole; be damned if I don't believe it's even the same mud."

"That was last year. There's more business now. So much more that I can't afford not to go up."

"All right, Goddammit," Boon said. "Go on." So we moved, ignominious, at the pace of the mules, on into the next mudhole without stopping, on and out again. The bridge was just ahead now; beyond it we could see the road all the way to the edge of the bottom and safety.

"You're all right now," the man said. "Until you come back." Boon was unhooking the log chain while Ned freed the traces and handed the doubletree back up to the man on the mule.

"We ain't coming back this way," Boon said.

"I wouldn't neither," the man said. Boon went back to the last puddle and washed some of the mud from his hands and came back and took four dollars from his wallet. The man didn't move.

"It's six dollars," he said.

"Last year it was two dollars," Boon said. "You said it's double now. Double two is four. All right. Here's four dollars."

"I charge a dollar a passenger," the man said. "There was two of you last year. That was two dollars. The price is doubled now. There's three of you. That's six dollars. Maybe you'd rather walk back to Jefferson than pay two dollars, but maybe that boy and that nigger wouldn't."

"And maybe I ain't gone up neither," Boon said. "Suppose I don't pay you six dollars. Suppose in fact I don't pay you nothing."

"You can do that too," the man said. "These mules has had a hard day, but I reckon there's still enough git in them to drag that thing back where they got it from."

But Boon had already quit, given up, surrendered. "Goddammit," he said, "this boy ain't nothing but a child! Sholy for just a little child——"

"Walking back to Jefferson might be lighter for him," the man said, "but it won't be no shorter."

"All right," Boon said, "but look at the other one! When he gets that mud washed off, he ain't even white!"

The man looked at distance awhile, then he looked at Boon. "Son," he said, "both these mules is color-blind."

(1962)

A Fine Piece of Machinery

By Everett Greenbaum

MY FATHER bought his Pierce-Arrow in 1926. The Pierce was one of the great cars of its day. It had huge headlight eyes growing right out of its fenders. Ours, with its twenty coats of deep-green lacquer, had a handsome, reptile look. It had a beautiful box of tools right on the running board; vases in the back where you could put cut flowers; and, on the cylinders, little brass priming cups into which you squirted gasoline to start the engine in cold weather.

"Now, there's a fine piece of machinery," my father would say, admiring it. Then he would sock one of the fenders, producing a dull thud.

"Aluminum!" he would say. The body was made of aluminum. The use of this metal for automobile bodies was a rare thing then. As a child I had a notion that they saved enough aluminum foil from chewing gum until they had enough to make a car, and that's why they cost so much.

My father really knew how to handle the Pierce. At stop signs he could make it play music by letting the clutch out a bit and shifting part way into gear. To play higher notes, he fed more gas to her. He could play "Button Up Your Overcoat" as far as "when the wind blows" but not as far as "free."

"Are you sure you're not hurting it?" my mother would say.

"You can't hurt a piece of engineering like this transmission," my father would say.

The older we got, the fonder he became of that car. And the older the Pierce got, the more ashamed of it Mama and the girls became. When we passed certain key locales in our hometown of Buffalo, New York, where it was necessary to make an impression, they would slump down so they wouldn't be seen. They went down on Nottingham Terrace and Delaware Ave-

nue, really hitting the floor when we passed Temple Beth Zion.

Each year when the new-model cars came out, my mother left folders around the house, hoping something modern would catch my father's eye. She hoped he'd buy a car like the ones she rode in with other ladies to mah-jongg afternoons or to the Fort Erie races.

He treated her automobile brochures with scorn. I remember the year the streamline Chrysler came out. My crowd thought it was terrific. My father stared at the folder. "Tin balloon!" he scoffed. He tore it up, throwing it into our gas fireplace among the fake logs and moss.

Certain events connected with the Pierce stand as signposts in my life. I must have been eight when it caught fire. It was one of Buffalo's cold, winter Sundays. We were getting ready to go to Sunday school. She wouldn't turn over. The oil was like molasses.

"Well, Ev, we'll have to prime her," my father said happily.

"We don't have a can of gasoline," I said.

"Don't matter, you'll just suck on that pipe there till she begins to siphon down, and we'll catch some."

"But, Daddy, I just had breakfast! What if I swallow the gasoline?" I said.

"Suck," he said.

For a moment I sucked unsuccessfully. Then a sudden rush of fuel gushed all over the engine. Since we had left the ignition switch on, it burst into flames.

"Fire alarm!" My father waved toward the red box on the corner.

Neighbors on their way to St. Mark's next door were astonished to see me rushing against them to get to the firebox. I broke the glass and pulled the thing. I had always wanted to.

When I got back, my father and the Catholics were throwing snowballs on the fire. It was only smoke by

then. When the firemen arrived, it was just a wisp of steam. The Pierce's hood was still a shiny, deep green.

"What a finish!" my father murmured.

But gasoline and corn flakes and sliced bananas were too much for a Sunday-school boy. As I went upstairs to throw up, I saw the females of our house watching everything from the dining-room window.

"Is the car all burned up, Mama?" my little sister asked.

"No, dammit!" my mother said.

I didn't have to go to Sunday school that time.

The Pierce saved me from Sunday school another time, too. As always, I was dressed earlier than the girls. I had on my itchy, navy-blue Sunday suit and my itchy, blue overcoat. Both suit and coat had horsehairs in the lapels to keep their shape. I must have had a hundred dollars' worth of horsehairs in that Sunday-school outfit.

I thought it would be a nice surprise for everybody if I got the Pierce out of the garage all by myself. I couldn't drive, being only nine, but I had a plan. I would push the car until she got rolling down the hill of the drive. Then I would dash around to the front seat, leap into the car, and slam on the brakes when it reached the sidewalk. That way, when my father and the girls came out of the house, there would be no tiresome getting that old car out of the garage. It would be a nice surprise.

I had to rock her several times. At first I thought she wouldn't go. But she did. She went like mad. She hurtled down the drive like sixty. The plan slipped out of my head. My only thought was to hang onto the bumper and stop that car. I was dragged like a dead mouse right down the drive, right through the Catholics, right into the street, where oncoming cars screeched their brakes.

The Pierce hit a large tree, which later turned brown. But it stopped. The front of my Sunday outfit completely shredded, I got to my feet. Naturally I was terribly embarrassed. I had climbed behind the wheel when my family appeared, openmouthed, on the veranda.

"It wasn't my fault," I said. "She got away from me."

I didn't have to go to Sunday school that time. Nor did I get to go to Shea's North Park Theatre for the next ten Saturdays.

Not too long after that, however, I saved the lives of our entire family in the line of automotive duty.

It was springtime. My father had decided that we would get in the car and drive to Cleveland to visit our

A prestige auto, the Pierce-Arrow was manufactured in Buffalo, 1903–1938, with "body of hand-hammered aluminum over white ash."

friends, the Alperins. We were still within the city when it began to snow. As sometimes happens around Buffalo in the spring, the storm developed into a blizzard. We slithered along the highway.

"Have to shift her into second now," my father said, double-clutching.

Things grew worse. The snow was falling so heavily and wetly that the Pierce's wipers couldn't budge it. We looked out at a dark gray wall.

"Good night, nurse! What are we going to do now?" my mother said.

"Ev," my father said, "you'll get up on that hood and keep those wipers clear."

I did. By the time we reached Lackawanna, where the street lights were lit and snowplows were working, I was frozen solid. But a Buffalo kid is frozen half the year anyhow; a little hot tomato soup thawed me out.

A lot of things connected with the Pierce seemed to happen on Sundays. It was on a Sunday that Mama and the girls really thought they'd got rid of the dragon-eyed car for good.

We went to Polonsky's restaurant for dinner on Sundays. Our favorite waitress there was called Honey. She had a mop of frizzled, peroxide hair. My father kidded her a lot to make her giggle. He would wait until the whole tremendous meal was finished and we were leaving, then he would turn to her and say, "Well, Honey, how about bringing me a nice bowl of soup?" She would die laughing.

This one particular Sunday, right after the soup joke, we got into the Pierce, which was right out front alongside the trolley tracks.

My father fired her up, ground her into low, and gave his cold-weather signal: one gloved finger sticking out of the barely opened window. We began to pull out.

"Watch out for the streetcar!" my mother said.

"We've got the right of way!" my father said.

The thing I remember most about the wreck was my astonishment at how much wood there was under the aluminum. It was all over the street. We were unhurt but shaking like Jewish leaves.

"I'll take care of the boy," someone said. It was Honey.

She took me into the ladies' room to pee pee. I hoped none of the kids would hear about this.

"Don't talk to anyone," my father ordered. "I'm going

Tire chains gave a noisy, bumpy ride but it was a ride—they kept cars moving. The only thing harder than putting them on was taking them off after the fasteners were clogged with ice. Between snowstorms you carried the chains in a canvas bag, where they rattled. (1925)

"Take your foot off the gas," Calver said. "You'll get more vacuum."

I did. The suction was fantastic. The tube became an angry little leech trying to inhale my skin. I heard a soft *pop* and watched a piece of nose go up the straw. Calver had the sense to turn the ignition off. He helped me into the house, blood running down my face.

"That car is a curse," my mother said.

How nice it would be to be able to say that the Pierce became my first "dating" car, to be able to tell of long moonlit rides along Lake Erie, with my arm around Ralpha Becker or Irene Egbert or even Claire Hochgrebe. But the Pierce left our family before I reached that stage of development.

Like many terrible things happening then, it was because of Hitler. War was getting close in Europe. The price of aluminum soared.

The car was stolen on a Thursday night while my father was having a sweat and rubdown at the Montefiore Club. The police thought the thief must have followed him for a couple of weeks to learn his habits.

No crime ever precipitated more phone calls. There were calls without letup: calls to detectives, desk sergeants, judges, and the Chief of Police.

Just before dawn Friday, an incoming call ended it all. We hung over the upstairs banister in our pajamas, listening. The Pierce had been found in the woods, stripped of her aluminum.

"No," my father said quietly, "no, no, I don't want to look at it." He hung up, and we all went to bed. We never really knew for certain, but for as long as she lived my mother stuck to the story that she had won fifty dollars at the Fort Erie track and had given it to two men to steal the Pierce-Arrow.   (1967)

to phone Bill Brock." He left to call his lawyer.

Well, Bill Brock handled the streetcar company all right, and, to my mother's anguish, the Pierce looked as good as new in three weeks.

"You can't kill the heart of a well-made machine," my father said.

As I reached adolescence, the Pierce got new piston rings and I got pimples. A lot of my friends had them, but I really hated mine. I determined to do something about them. I decided that a pimple was nothing more or less than some foreign substance under the skin. If you could get that right out of there, the pimple then had no reason to exist and would go away.

The Pierce had a vacuum-operated windshield wiper. When the engine was running, you could slip the rubber hose off and actually feel that strong suction. If you put a lighted cigarette in the hose, it got smoked in a jiffy right in front of your eyes; my friend Calver Oakes and I did it often.

Here was the answer to my skin problem. I got hold of a glass straw and waited for a good pimple to show up. Sure enough, one did, right on the nose. But Calver and I weren't going to rush things. We held the glass straw under the hot-water spigot until we were sure it was sterile. Then we went out to the Pierce, put the unsanitary end of the glass straw on the hose and the sanitary end on my nose. Then I started the engine and stepped on the gas. It drew nicely.

The Accident

By Jesse Stuart

"HOW WOULD YOU LIKE TO GO FOR A RIDE with your Aunt Effie and me?" Uncle Jad said. "It's a nice Sunday afternoon and we won't have many more such days before snow falls."

Uncle Jad Higgins ran the Ranceburg Men's Clothing Store in Ranceburg. He had inherited this store from his father, and there was a sign above the door which read: SEVENTY-SEVEN YEARS IN BUSINESS. The Higginses were without posterity, and I was Uncle Jad's sister's son; it was understood that I would take over the store someday after Uncle Jad retired or was deceased. Since my father was a farmer, Uncle Jad had invited me to live with him and Aunt Effie while learning the business from A to Z, and of course I couldn't let an opportunity like that pass. Naturally, if Uncle Jad asked me to do something, I did it. If he wanted me to take a drive with him and Aunt Effie on a sunny fall afternoon, I went along. I'd seen enough of the Lantern County hills to do me a lifetime, but if they wanted me with them, then that was all right with me.

"It's a nice idea to take a drive, Uncle Jad," I said. "You are so right. We won't have many more afternoons as pretty and as sunny as this one."

"Yes, and your Aunt Effie and I have seen more seasons—winters, springs, summers, autumns—than we will ever see again," he said.

"The years take their toll. But it's always nice just to get out and drive around."

"You want me to drive so you and Aunt Effie can relax and look at the countryside?" I asked.

"No, Tom, I'd rather have my own hands on the steering wheel," he said. "You know I have faith in you. But this is just my nature. I've never had a wreck in my life. And I've been driving since I was sixteen."

Aunt Effie came into the room dressed like she was going to church. Aunt Effie was a big woman, with twinkling blue eyes. She was always smiling and she always had something to say. She dressed in the latest style, wearing big hats and dresses with frills and laces. No wonder Uncle Jad and Aunt Effie were considered the best-dressed couple in Lantern County. They spent a lot of money for clothes, and took plenty of time getting properly dressed for an occasion. Uncle Jad warned me about wearing the right clothes when I took over his store after he was gone. He said I'd be selling men's clothes, and young men would be watching what I wore, so I'd have to be a living example of the well-dressed man. Uncle Jad was himself a living example of the well-dressed man in Lantern County.

Uncle Jad was not tall, and he was big around the middle and little on each end, which made him hard to fit, but he wore the kind of clothes that made him look good. He wore small hats with broad brims, and pinstripe suits to give him height. On this particular fall Sunday afternoon he wore a pair of gloves, not because he'd need them in the car, but just to accent the positive. He never missed a trick when it came to wearing clothes or selling them. He wouldn't wear a pair of shoes out of his own house onto the porch unless they were shined.

"Effie, you look real well," Uncle Jad said. "You look real nice in that blue suit and that white blouse with the lace collar. It's most appropriate for early winter wear."

"Well, Poppie, *you* look wonderful," she complimented him. "Yes, I've got the most handsome man in Lantern County." She pulled him over to her and kissed him. She was always very affectionate with Uncle Jad.

Well, they were telling each other the truth with their compliments, I thought as they walked toward the garage. I got ahead of them and raised the garage door. Then Uncle Jad opened the car door for Aunt Effie and, after she got in, pushed the door shut gently behind her. Then he walked around to the other side, got in, started the engine, and backed the car out. He waited for me to pull the garage door back down and get in the back seat. This was our regular routine.

"Well, which way shall we go, Mother?" he asked Aunt Effie.

"Let's drive up Kinney Creek Valley and over to Taysville," she replied quickly. Aunt Effie always knew where she wanted to go. All Uncle Jad had to do, if he was undecided, was to ask. She could soon make a decision.

"Then up Kinney Valley and over to Taysville we will go," Uncle Jad said.

"The valley will be beautiful this time of year," I said. "I am glad, Aunt Effie, that you have chosen this route. There'll still be autumn leaves on many of the oaks."

"You are so right," Aunt Effie said.

Uncle Jad drove slowly and carefully down the street. When he came to the railway crossing at the edge of Ranceburg, he stopped and looked carefully this way and that, though he could see for a mile either up or down the tracks.

"It always pays to be careful," he said. "Never had a wreck or hit a person. I can certainly boast of my record."

"I've not been driving very long, Uncle Jad," I said. "But I've never hit a person or had a wreck either."

"You're a careful young man, Tom," he said. "That is why I'm turning everything over to you someday. You're a lot like my father and me. By looks and by nature you could well have been my son!"

"Thank you, Uncle Jad," I said.

"I've got security in life," he said. "Mother and I could live to the end of our days without my working anymore. Mother and I have had a good life. We go to our church, vote for our party, belong to a few organizations. We are somebody in Ranceburg now, and remember, Tom, it *pays* in this life to be somebody. So be a somebody when your Aunt Effie and I are no longer around. Marry a nice woman. Drive a nice car and wear good clothes. Make your life a safe adventure."

We were in Kinney Valley now. There had been a few killing frosts, and the grass on the pasture fields was brown, but the oaks in the wooded areas were still filled with multicolored leaves. As we passed farmhouse after farmhouse, Uncle Jad called out the name of the man who lived there, and told how many sons he had and if

For many families the Sunday afternoon drive into the country was ritual. On such an expedition one admired the scenery, the crops, other cars.

they traded at the store. Uncle Jad also mentioned which men he had to ask for cash, and which could be trusted to buy now and pay later.

There were green areas on the Kinney Valley bottoms where winter wheat had been sown. When the wind swept through the valley, the wheat bent and rose up again after the wind had passed. The sun was bright, and when a crow flew over, though we didn't always see the crow, we could tell where he was flying by his shadow on the brown grass of the fields.

"Life is just so wonderful, Poppie," Aunt Effie said with enthusiasm. And she put her arm around Uncle Jad's neck, pulled him over, and kissed his cheek.

"Do be careful, Mother," Uncle Jad said. "You could cause me to have my first wreck." Actually, he liked for her to do him this way. He was just pretending that it could be dangerous.

"Yes, I have a fine automobile, fine store, fine home, prettiest wife in Ranceburg," Uncle Jad said. "When a man gets old enough to have security and enjoy life, the

World War II put an end to this pleasant custom. Under wartime gas rationing people had to hoard precious gallons for more necessary trips.

tragedy is he's about old enough to die and leave this world. Not a very pleasant thought, but how true it is!"

If life could shape up for me, I thought, like it had shaped up for Uncle Jad and Aunt Effie, then I'd be a happy man. They had everything they wanted. They had security. And they would go to the end of their days like this!

"Look out, Poppie!" Aunt Effie screamed, and covered her face with her hands. Uncle Jad slammed on the brakes. The car skidded, the tires squealed, and there was a thud. I saw a man fly up and hit a tree.

"Where did he come from?" Uncle Jad said. "I didn't see him until he was in front of the car."

"I saw just as you hit him!" I shouted.

"I wonder if I killed him," Uncle Jad said. His face was extremely white. He had lost that redness of color that made his cheeks pink. He sat with his hands on the steering wheel, looking out of the car at the man who lay at the foot of a large oak close to the highway.

"Oh, Poppie!" Aunt Effie wailed. She kept her hands

On America's Main Streets one shopped for men's clothing in one store, ladies' in another. For other necessities there were dry goods and hardware stores. One parked at the curb (no meters). The advent of chain stores, then shopping centers, changed this pleasant pattern.

over her face. "We bragged too soon! Life has been too good. We couldn't go on until the end with all this good fortune we have been having."

"He's not dead," Uncle Jad said. "He's trying to raise his head up to see what has happened. He's looking at the car. The poor fellow is looking at me! He's looking at me and trying to smile."

When Uncle Jad got out of the car, I got out with him.

"I never saw you," Uncle Jad told the man. "I'm sorry. How bad are you hurt?"

"I don't know," he answered softly. "Lift me upon my feet."

Uncle Jad got on one side and I got on the other, and we lifted him up. The man put his arms around our shoulders.

"See if you can bear your weight," Uncle Jad said.

The man tried one foot and then the other, and took two steps.

"Thank God!" Uncle Jad said. "No broken legs."

"It knocked the wind from me," the man said. "It jarred me to my foundations!"

Well, I knew that the big car had done that much and more too. The man had hit the side of the tree about six feet up and then fallen to the ground in a crumpled mass of humanity. Such a lick should have killed him outright.

"What is your name?" Uncle Jad asked.

"Mort Simmons." He sighed softly. "I'm John Simmons' boy."

He was a less-than-average-sized man who looked like he weighed about 130. He was wearing a work shirt and jeans, and brush-scarred brogan shoes without socks. His face was unshaven, with a growth of stubbly black beard.

"And where do you live?" Uncle Jad asked.

"On Shelf's Fork of Kinney."

"I thought I knew about everybody in Lantern County," Uncle Jad said, "but I'm sorry to say I don't know you or your father. Have you ever traded in my store in Ranceburg?"

"No, but I will in the future," the man replied.

"Poppie, let's take him to Doctor Raike and have him checked," Aunt Effie said.

"Not a bad idea, Mother," Uncle Jad said, and sighed. We helped Mort Simmons to the car. When we took his arms from around our shoulders, he stood up all right, and although we helped him to get on the rear seat, I think he could have done it by himself.

"I feel much better," he said.

"What about going back to Ranceburg with us and letting Doctor Raike see you before we take you home?" Uncle Jad asked him.

"That will be all right," he said. "Yes, I'd like to go see how bad I'm hurt."

"You watch over him now, Tom," Uncle Jad told me.

In a small town store like Uncle Jad's a boy was likely to be fitted with his first long pants by the man who had fitted his father's, years before. J. C. Leyendecker painted this 1937 Post *cover of smiles, tears.*

The caption that appeared with this picture in a 1936 advertisement: "Mister, I'm going to own a Buick, too, when I grow up."

"If he gets dizzy he might just pitch over! Watch him!"

"I will, Uncle Jad," I said as I got in the car. "Don't you worry!"

"No, I've got a lot to worry about now," he said.

Aunt Effie, who couldn't stand much excitement, was trembling like a leaf on a November oak. Uncle Jad was still pale, and his hands shook so on the steering wheel that the car swerved back and forth. But there was very little traffic on the country roads this time of year, and we made it safely back to Dr. Raike's office in Ranceburg.

"I'm glad you are here, Doctor Raike," Uncle Jad said. "I hit this man and knocked him upon the side of an oak tree. I never saw him until my car hit him. Seems like he just came up out of the ground. Mort Simmons. You ever have him for a patient before?"

"Can't say that I have," Dr. Raike said. "No, I don't know that name Simmons in Lantern County."

Dr. Raike, who was almost as old as my Uncle Jad,

was a little man with blue eyes and a kind face. He had once had golden blond hair, but time had turned it white.

"I'm John Simmons' boy, and we live on Shelf's Fork of Kinney Valley," Mort Simmons said.

"Well, I wouldn't know all the people who live on Kinney Valley anymore," Dr. Raike said. "Now, let me see about you."

Dr. Raike went over Mort Simmons' head and arms and legs. Then he had Mort strip off his shirt so that his back could be examined.

"You've been shaken up," Dr. Raike said, "and you've got a lot of minor bruises. But you don't have any broken bones. I can release you, all right."

"Doc, how much do I owe you?" Uncle Jad asked.

"Not anything, Jad," Dr. Raike said. "Glad to do it. I hope everything will be all right for you."

"Thank you, Doc," Uncle Jad said, with a worried look.

The good life in 1931: a fine car (this one is an Oldsmobile) and a fine day for "getting away" into the country. The motorist was pleasantly isolated from the tedium and trials of life, before the advent of car radios, CBs and Sunday afternoon traffic jams.

Mort Simmons walked out of the office under his own power, though he limped and moved his legs very stiffly, and Uncle Jad wasn't as nervous on the drive back to Kinney Valley as he had been when he drove Mort in to Ranceburg. He had more self-composure.

"Let me out here," Mort Simmons said at last. "You can't drive up Shelf's Fork. The road is too bad. I don't want you to hurt your fine car."

"Sure you can make it all right?" Uncle Jad asked. "I'll try to take you on. I don't mind hurting my car."

"I can make it," Mort Simmons said. "Thank you for taking me to the doctor, and thank you for bringing me back."

"I'm so sorry this happened," Uncle Jad said. "I truly am."

Mort Simmons smiled and walked up a narrow little slit of a road alongside a small stream. Uncle Jad drove back toward Ranceburg.

"Well, Mother, our pleasant Sunday afternoon didn't turn out too well," he said. "It seems like I've dreamed what has happened! But when I wake up in the morn-

ing, I'll know it *did* happen. We might be sued for everything we have. We might not have any more security in this life."

"See John as soon as we get back," Aunt Effie said.

"John Lovell is a good lawyer," Uncle Jad said. "I'm glad we have him."

He asked Aunt Effie and me if either of us had seen where Mort Simmons came from at the time of the accident, and we said we never saw him until he was in front of the car and it was making contact with his body.

"I'd just climbed a rise," Uncle Jad said. "I wasn't going fast. If I had been going fast, he wouldn't have known what struck him. I am a lucky man."

"It's worked out for the best," Aunt Effie said. "I believe what is to be will be."

That evening Uncle Jad told John Lovell what had happened and how it had happened. John Lovell said that one bit of luck Uncle Jad would have if he were sued was that he would have two witnesses while Mort Simmons would only have himself. Uncle Jad told John Lovell how pleasant the man was and about his good manners. He told how Mort Simmons had been thankful for being taken to Dr. Raike and examined, and for being brought back to the Shelf's Fork road that led to his home. But John Lovell admonished Uncle Jad that Mort Simmons might nevertheless be thinking he had a good chance to sue, for everybody in Lantern Valley was pretty sure Uncle Jad had plenty of money.

When Uncle Jad came back from the lawyer's house, he told Aunt Effie about how he had been warned, and that night he was so worried he had to take medicine to put himself to sleep. The next morning he said to Aunt Effie, "Mother, yesterday is still a bad dream."

"I can't believe it either," she said. "But all three of us know that it *did* happen."

After breakfast Uncle Jad and I walked to the store, only two blocks away. We always opened at seven to catch the early-morning trade of men on their way to work. It didn't seem like anything special was going to happen that day, but that afternoon I looked out of the office at the back of the store and saw Mort Simmons looking at some shirts. "See what he wants," Uncle Jad said when I told him.
"I'll stay out of the way.

I think I know what he wants. He wants to know more about this business before he sues me."

I went out to Mort Simmons and said with a smile, "Good afternoon." He smiled and said, "Howdy." Then he said, "I've come for some work shirts. We've been working in the tobacco, and I've got glue from the tobacco on all my shirts. I want a couple of clean shirts to go against my body. But I can't pay you until tomorrow. Our tobacco sells today in Taysville, and Pa will fetch the money home. So I'll pay you tomorrow, if that will be all right?"

"It will be all right," I said.

I knew Uncle Jad was in the back listening, and I knew he wouldn't want me to contrary Mort Simmons. I hoped I was doing things the right way, and decided that I would make the debt good if it didn't get paid.

I showed Mort Simmons all the work shirts we had, and he ended up buying two, size fifteen with a thirty-two-inch sleeve length. He smiled when he left, and I smiled and thanked him for purchasing in this store. When Mort Simmons was gone, Uncle Jad came out of the little office where he had kept himself hidden.

"You played it just right," he said. "You are a good diplomat, Tom! I feel sure he's going to sue, but it doesn't hurt to soften him up. We've let him know how friendly we are. We have built our business here because the people know we are friendly and reliable. We serve the public! And this will be the first time a Higgins has ever been sued. My father before me, Abraham Higgins, was never sued. And I have never been sued."

"I can't figure that man out," I said.

"Well, I can't either," Uncle Jad said. "But I don't think he will be back to pay for the shirts. I think this is the last time we will see him before he sues me. The friendly man that looks at you and smiles and asks some little favor, that is the man who will sue you quicker than you can bat your eye."

At home that evening we told Aunt Effie what had happened, and Aunt Effie, who had always been good at judging people, said she didn't know what to think. She said she was puzzled. The next day went along very quietly until the early afternoon. I was restacking some shirts when I turned around, and there stood Mort Simmons again. I looked back and saw Uncle Jad scurrying into his office.

"Pa is here with me," Mort Simmons said. "And four of my brothers have come too."

I thought I was going to sink through the

Small-town cop, comfortable but on the alert for traffic law violators, painted for a 1929 Post *cover.*

floor! His father and his brothers! They had come for Uncle Jad and me! It ran through my mind that this was the way with the people who lived among the high hills and in the deep hollows. Do something to one, even if it is an accident, and his blood kin will never stop harassing you as long as you live. Uncle Jad and I were in a lot of trouble!

"We've come to get some orders filled," Mort Simmons said. "It's shoe and clothes time before winter sets in."

"All right," I said.

"Come and meet Mr. John Simmons, my pa, and my four brothers," he said.

I said hello to the five big men standing over by the door. And then I filled the biggest order I had ever filled for one family since I came to work in Uncle Jad's store. They took two pairs of shoes each; they took socks, underwear, handkerchiefs, work pants, work shirts and Sunday shirts. And all five brothers picked out suits. I handed out almost five hundred dollars' worth of clothes and shoes, and I was sure there would be no mention of paying till Mort Simmons got through suing Uncle Jad.

After they had everything, John Simmons said to me, "Where is your uncle? I would like to see him."

Here it comes, I thought. I knew that Uncle Jad couldn't run from trouble. He would have to meet this Simmons family and tell them he had an attorney to represent him. They would have to consult his attorney. Or his attorney could talk to them.

I went back to the office and told Uncle Jad that John Simmons and his sons were asking for him, and that they had ordered almost five hundred dollars' worth of merchandise.

Uncle Jad's face lost its color just like it had when his car hit Mort Simmons and flung him upon the side of the big oak.

"Guess I'll have to go and face them," he said. "You with me, Tom?"

We went back to where the Simmonses were standing with bundles of merchandise in their arms, and more bundles around them on the floor. Uncle Jad was shaking. His lips were twitching nervously, and he kept jerking his head.

"Mr. Higgins, I wanted to meet you," John Simmons said. "You are a fine man. That's the reason my son Mort was in here yesterday. And that's why I brought my other sons here today to get new Sunday suits and winter clothes and shoes."

"Thank you, Mr. Simmons," Uncle Jad stammered. He couldn't understand why he was being called a fine man.

"We've got our tobacco money now," John Simmons said. "No charging anything. Here is what we owe you, including the cost of those shirts Mort bought yesterday."

Uncle Jad and I stood there, so surprised we couldn't speak, and John Simmons handed over the money, every cent. "As I have said, Mr. Higgins," he said, "we know from what happened last Sunday that you are a fine man."

"Last Sunday? You mean the accident?" Uncle Jad was still stammering.

"It was not the kind of accident you mean," John Simmons corrected him. "You see, my son Mort has a fault. He's as absent-minded as can be, never thinks what he's doing or looks where he is going. I have warned him many times about that fault, but he keeps walking out in front of cars, and he tells me he just can't think why it's so hard for him to remember not to do it. He will be marked by a car one of these days."

Uncle Jad was beginning to recover himself. Color was beginning to come back into his face.

"You see, Mr. Higgins," John Simmons said, "my son Mort has been struck by cars half a dozen times, and you're the only man who ever picked him up, took him to the doctor, and was even nice enough to fetch him back toward his home. I just want you to know that his mother and I appreciate what you did. And buying from you is a good way to thank you. We will be back to trade with you from now on. Thank you."

Uncle Jad and I shook hands with all the Simmonses, and they smiled and we smiled. I have known my Uncle Jad since I was a little boy big enough to remember anything. And I never saw him so happy as he was right then, though he still had a puzzled look on his face.

(1966)

Of the cars shown in color on this and the following pages only the Cadillac is still manufactured. The Packard lingered until 1958 but all the others disappeared by 1940, victims of the Great Depression that came after the extravagant era Fitzgerald described. Above, a 1930 Willys-Knight sedan.

Gatsby's Party

By F. Scott Fitzgerald

Millions of words have been written about the Jazz Age but the definitive portrait is still to be found in The Great Gatsby. *Here is the real thing, for Fitzgerald was describing the contemporary scene (the book was published in 1925) and the social circle in which he moved. Here are the people who drove—or were driven in, behind uniformed chauffeurs—some of the most beautiful cars ever built. Though every second car on the road was one of Henry Ford's black Model T's, Fitzgerald's characters traveled in style, in sleek long-hooded limousines and in jaunty roadsters hand-lacquered in Easter-egg pastels.*

The name Cadillac survives, but it is borne today by automobiles that would appear modest parked beside this 1929 town car.

THERE WAS MUSIC from my neighbor's house through the summer nights. In his blue gardens men and girls came and went like moths among the whisperings and the champagne and the stars. At high tide in the afternoon I watched his guests diving from the tower of his raft or taking the sun on the hot sand of his beach while his two motorboats slit the waters of the Sound, drawing aquaplanes over cataracts of foam. On weekends his Rolls-Royce became an omnibus, bearing parties to and from the city between nine in the morning and long past midnight, while his station wagon scampered like a brisk yellow bug to meet all trains. And on Mondays eight servants, including an extra gardener, toiled all day with mops and scrubbing-brushes and hammers and garden-shears, repairing the ravages of the night before.

Every Friday five crates of oranges and lemons arrived from a fruiterer in New York—every Monday these same oranges and lemons left his back door in a pyramid of pulpless halves. There was a machine in the kitchen which could extract the juice of two hundred oranges in half an hour if a little button was pressed two hundred times by a butler's thumb.

At least once a fortnight a corps of caterers came down with several hundred feet of canvas and enough colored lights to make a Christmas tree of Gatsby's enormous garden. On buffet tables, garnished with glistening hors-d'oeuvre, spiced baked hams crowded against salads of harlequin designs and pastry pigs and turkeys bewitched to a dark gold. In the main hall a bar with a real brass rail was set up, and stocked with gins and liquors and with cordials so long forgotten that most of his female guests were too young to know one from another.

By seven o'clock the orchestra has arrived, no thin five-piece affair, but a whole pitful of oboes and trombones and saxophones and viols and cornets and piccolos, and low and high drums. The last swimmers have come in from the beach now and are dressing upstairs; the cars from New York are parked five deep in the drive, and already the halls and salons and verandas are gaudy with primary colors, and hair shorn in strange new ways, and shawls beyond the dreams of Castile. The bar is in full swing, and floating rounds of cocktails permeate the garden outside, until the air is alive with chatter and laughter, and casual innuendo and introductions forgotten on the spot, and enthusiastic meetings between women who never knew each other's names.

The lights grow brighter as the earth lurches away from the sun, and now the orchestra is playing yellow cocktail music, and the opera of voices pitches a key higher. Laughter is easier minute by minute, spilled with prodigality, tipped out at a cheerful word. The groups change more swiftly, swell with new arrivals, dissolve and form in the same breath; already there are wanderers, confident girls who weave here and there among the stouter and more stable, become for a sharp, joyous moment the center of a group; and then, excited with triumph, glide on through the sea-change of faces and voices and color under the constantly changing light.

Suddenly one of these gypsies, in trembling opal, seizes a cocktail out of the air, dumps it down for cour-

"Gee, our old LaSalle ran great; those were the days," sing Edith and Archie Bunker in the theme song of "All in the Family." Actually the LaSalle was a luxury car, introduced in 1927 as a companion to the Cadillac. Shown here, a 1927 LaSalle appropriate for Gatsby's lifestyle, not Bunker's.

age and, moving her hands like Frisco, dances out alone on the canvas platform. A momentary hush; the orchestra leader varies his rhythm obligingly for her, and there is a burst of chatter as the erroneous news goes around that she is Gilda Gray's understudy from the Follies. The party has begun.

I believe that on the first night I went to Gatsby's house I was one of the few guests who had actually been invited. People were not invited—they went there. They got into automobiles which bore them out to Long Island, and somehow they ended up at Gatsby's door. Once there they were introduced by somebody who knew Gatsby, and after that they conducted themselves according to the rules of behavior associated with amusement parks. Sometimes they came and went without having met Gatsby at all, came for the party with a simplicity of heart that was its own ticket of admission.

I had been actually invited. A chauffeur in a uniform of robin's-egg blue crossed my lawn early that Saturday morning with a surprisingly formal note from his employer: the honor would be entirely Gatsby's, it said, if I would attend his "little party" that night. He had seen me several times, and had intended to call on me long before, but a peculiar combination of circumstances had prevented it—signed Jay Gatsby, in a majestic hand.

Dressed up in white flannels I went over to his lawn a little after seven, and wandered around rather ill at ease among swirls and eddies of people I didn't know—though here and there was a face I had noticed on the commuting train. I was immediately struck by the number of young Englishmen dotted about; all well dressed, all looking a little hungry, and all talking in low, earnest voices to solid and prosperous Americans. I was sure that they were selling something: bonds or insurance or automobiles. They were at least agonizingly aware of the easy money in the vicinity and convinced that it was theirs for a few words in the right key.

As soon as I arrived I made an attempt to find my

The old family retainer who carried one's bags and held open the gate was still a part of the picture of gracious living in 1927 (opposite page) and in 1930. When did he disappear? Before 1940, surely. The uniformed maid and chauffeur lingered a little longer, but after December 7, 1941, they were an endangered species.

Looking exactly as Fitzgerald's fictional Gatsby should look, Al Jolson posed in 1930 with his magnificent Mercedes. Note Jolson's white flannels and two-tone shoes, and the car's snugly buckled leather belt. The splendid automobile was part and parcel of the Hollywood lifestyle at the time Jolson, star of 1927's The Jazz Singer, *was riding high.*

host, but the two or three people of whom I asked his whereabouts stared at me in such an amazed way, and denied so vehemently any knowledge of his movements, that I slunk off in the direction of the cocktail table—the only place in the garden where a single man could linger without looking purposeless and alone.

I was on my way to get roaring drunk from sheer embarrassment when Jordan Baker came out of the house and stood at the head of the marble steps, leaning a little backward and looking with contemptuous interest down into the garden.

Welcome or not, I found it necessary to attach myself to someone before I should begin to address cordial remarks to the passersby.

"Hello!" I roared, advancing toward her. My voice seemed unnaturally loud across the garden.

"I thought you might be here," she responded absently as I came up, "I remembered you lived next door to——"

She held my hand impersonally, as a promise that she'd take care of me in a minute, and gave ear to two girls in twin yellow dresses, who stopped at the foot of the steps.

"Hello!" they cried together. "Sorry you didn't win."

That was for the golf tournament. She had lost in the finals the week before.

"You don't know who we are," said one of the girls in yellow, "but we met you here about a month ago."

"You've dyed your hair since then," remarked Jordan, and I started, but the girls had moved casually on and her remark was addressed to the premature moon, produced like the supper, no doubt, out of a caterer's basket. With Jordan's slender golden arm resting in mine, we descended the steps and sauntered about the garden. A tray of cocktails floated at us through the twilight, and we sat down at a table with the two girls in yellow and three men, each one introduced as Mr. Mumble.

"Do you come to these parties often?" inquired Jordan of the girl beside her.

"The last one was the one I met you at," answered the girl, in an alert confident voice. She turned to her companion: "Wasn't it for you, Lucille?"

It was for Lucille, too.

"I like to come," Lucille said. "I never care what I do, so I always have a good time. When I was here last I tore my gown on a chair, and he asked me my name and address—inside of a week I got a package from Croirier's with a new evening gown in it."

"Did you keep it?" asked Jordan.

"Sure I did. I was going to wear it tonight, but it was too big in the bust and had to be altered. It was gas blue with lavender beads. Two hundred and sixty-five dollars."

"There's something funny about a fellow that'll do a thing like that," said the other girl eagerly. "He doesn't want any trouble with *any*body."

"Who doesn't?" I inquired.

"Gatsby. Somebody told me——"

The two girls and Jordan leaned together confidentially.

"Somebody told me they thought he killed a man once."

A thrill passed over all of us. The three Mr. Mumbles bent forward and listened eagerly.

"I don't think it's so much *that*," argued Lucille skeptically; "it's more that he was a German spy during the war."

One of the men nodded in confirmation.

"I heard that from a man who knew all about him, grew up with him in Germany," he assured us positively.

"Oh, no," said the first girl, "it couldn't be that, because he was in the American army during the war." As our credulity switched back to her she leaned forward with enthusiasm. "You look at him sometimes when he thinks nobody's looking at him. I'll bet he killed a man."

She narrowed her eyes and shivered. Lucille shivered. We all turned and looked around for Gatsby. It was testimony to the romantic speculation he inspired that there were whispers about him from those who had found little that it was necessary to whisper about in this world.

The first supper—there would be another one after midnight—was now being served, and Jordan invited me to join her own party, who were spread around a table on the other side of the garden. There were three married couples and Jordan's escort, a persistent undergraduate given to violent innuendo, and obviously under the impression that sooner or later Jordan was going to yield him up her person to a greater or lesser degree. Instead of rambling this party had preserved a dignified homogeneity, and assumed to itself the function of representing the staid nobility of the countryside—East Egg condescending to West Egg, carefully on guard against spectroscopic gaiety.

This 1928 Essex belonged to a world of new fashions (cloche hats, dresses belted at the hipline), new kinds of music (ragtime, jazz), new heroes (Lindbergh, Babe Ruth, Douglas Fairbanks). Stock prices soared and Herbert Hoover defeated Al Smith in the presidential election of that year.

"Let's get out," whispered Jordan, after a somehow wasteful and inappropriate half-hour; "this is much too polite for me."

We got up, and she explained that we were going to find the host: I had never met him, she said, and it was making me uneasy. The undergraduate nodded in a cynical, melancholy way.

The bar, where we glanced first, was crowded, but Gatsby was not there. She couldn't find him from the top of the steps, and he wasn't on the veranda. On a chance we tried an important-looking door, and walked into a high Gothic library, paneled with carved English oak, and probably transported complete from some ruin overseas.

A stout, middle-aged man, with enormous owl-eyed spectacles, was sitting somewhat drunk on the edge of a great table, staring with unsteady concentration at the shelves of books. As we entered he wheeled excitedly around and examined Jordan from head to foot.

"What do you think?" he demanded impetuously.

"About what?"

He waved his hand toward the bookshelves.

"About that. As a matter of fact you needn't bother to ascertain. I ascertained. They're real."

"The books?"

He nodded.

"Absolutely real—have pages and everything. I thought they'd be a nice durable cardboard. Matter of

fact, they're absolutely real. Pages and— Here! Lemme show you."

Taking our skepticism for granted, he rushed to the bookcases and returned with Volume One of the "Stoddard Lectures."

"See!" he cried triumphantly. "It's a bona-fide piece of printed matter. It fooled me. This fella's a regular Belasco. It's a triumph. What thoroughness! What realism! Knew when to stop, too—didn't cut the pages. But what do you want? What do you expect?"

He snatched the book from me and replaced it hastily on its shelf, muttering that if one brick was removed the whole library was liable to collapse.

"Who brought you?" he demanded. "Or did you just come? I was brought. Most people were brought."

Jordan looked at him alertly, cheerfully, without answering.

"I was brought by a woman named Roosevelt," he continued. "Mrs. Claud Roosevelt. Do you know her? I met her somewhere last night. I've been drunk for about a week now, and I thought it might sober me up to sit in a library."

"Has it?"

"A little bit, I think. I can't tell yet. I've only been here an hour. Did I tell you about the books? They're real. They're——"

"You told us."

We shook hands with him gravely and went back outdoors.

There was dancing now on the canvas in the garden; old men pushing young girls backward in eternal graceless circles, superior couples holding each other tortuously, fashionably, and keeping in the corners—and a great number of single girls dancing individualistically or relieving the orchestra for a moment of the burden of the banjo or the traps. By midnight the hilarity had increased. A celebrated tenor had sung in Italian, and a notorious contralto had sung in jazz, and between the numbers people were doing "stunts" all over the garden, while happy, vacuous bursts of laughter rose toward the summer sky. A pair of stage twins, who turned out to be the girls in yellow, did a baby act in costume, and champagne was served in glasses bigger than finger-bowls. The moon had risen higher, and floating in the Sound was a triangle of silver scales, trembling a little to the stiff, tinny drip of the banjoes on the lawn.

I was still with Jordan Baker. We were sitting at a table with a man of about my age and a rowdy little girl, who gave way upon the slightest provocation to uncontrollable laughter. I was enjoying myself now. I had

"Some things are fundamentally beautiful of line. The Grecian pillar is one. The Packard is another." (1934 advertisement)

*By 1929 women were smoking
in public—and some were wearing
strange new garments called beach pajamas.
The car: a Hupmobile.*

By 1929 a girl could appear in a low-cut, form-fitting swimsuit without being arrested, as some had been in 1922. The car: a Franklin.

taken two fingerbowls of champagne, and the scene had changed before my eyes into something significant, elemental, and profound.

At a lull in the entertainment the man looked at me and smiled.

"Your face is familiar," he said, politely. "Weren't you in the Third Division during the war?"

"Why, yes. I was in the ninth machine-gun battalion."

"I was in the Seventh Infantry until June nineteen-eighteen. I knew I'd seen you somewhere before."

We talked for a moment about some wet, gray little villages in France. Evidently he lived in this vicinity, for he told me that he had just bought a hydroplane, and was going to try it out in the morning.

"Want to go with me, old sport? Just near the shore along the Sound."

"What time?"

"Any time that suits you best."

It was on the tip of my tongue to ask his name when Jordan looked around and smiled.

"Having a gay time now?" she inquired.

"Much better." I turned again to my new acquaintance. "This is an unusual party for me. I haven't even seen the host. I live over there—" I waved my hand at the invisible hedge in the distance, "and this man Gatsby sent over his chauffeur with an invitation."

For a moment he looked at me as if he failed to understand.

"I'm Gatsby," he said suddenly.

"What!" I exclaimed. "Oh, I beg your pardon."

"I thought you knew, old sport. I'm afraid I'm not a very good host."

He smiled understandingly—much more than understandingly. It was one of those rare smiles with a quality of eternal reassurance in it, that you may come across four or five times in life. It faced—or seemed to face—the whole external world for an instant, and then concentrated on *you* with an irresistible prejudice in your favor. It understood you just as far as you wanted to be understood, believed in you as you would like to believe in yourself, and assured you that it had precisely the impression of you that, at your best, you hoped to convey. Precisely at that point it vanished—and I was looking at an elegant young roughneck, a year or two over thirty, whose elaborate formality of speech just missed being absurd. Some time before he introduced himself I'd got a strong impression that he was picking his words with care.

Another new fashion of 1929—the uneven hemline that ranged from knee to ankle as if the designer couldn't make up his mind. The Empire State Building and Rockefeller Center were under construction and by one estimate there were 32,000 speakeasies in New York City. The car: a Franklin.

Almost at the moment when Mr. Gatsby identified himself a butler hurried toward him with the information that Chicago was calling him on the wire. He excused himself with a small bow that included each of us in turn.

"If you want anything just ask for it, old sport," he urged me. "Excuse me. I will rejoin you later."

When he was gone I turned immediately to Jordan—constrained to assure her of my surprise. I had expected that Mr. Gatsby would be a florid and corpulent person in his middle years.

"Who is he?" I demanded. "Do you know?"

"He's just a man named Gatsby."

"Where is he from, I mean? And what does he do?"

"Now *you're* started on the subject," she answered with a wan smile. "Well, he told me once he was an Oxford man."

A dim background started to take shape behind him, but at her next remark it faded away.

"However, I don't believe it."

"Why not?"

"I don't know," she insisted, "I just don't think he went there."

Something in her tone reminded me of the other girl's "I think he killed a man," and had the effect of stimulating my curiosity. I would have accepted without question the information that Gatsby sprang from the swamps of Louisiana or from the lower East Side of New York. That was comprehensible. But young men didn't—at least in my provincial inexperience I believed they didn't—drift coolly out of nowhere and buy a palace on Long Island Sound.

"Anyhow, he gives large parties," said Jordan, changing the subject with an urban distaste for the concrete. "And I like large parties. They're so intimate. At small parties there isn't any privacy."

There was the boom of a bass drum, and the voice of the orchestra leader rang out suddenly above the echolalia of the garden.

"Ladies and gentlemen," he cried. "At the request of Mr. Gatsby we are going to play for you Mr. Vladimir Tostoff's latest work, which attracted so much attention at Carnegie Hall last May. If you read the papers you know there was a big sensation." He smiled with jovial condescension, and added: "Some sensation!" Whereupon everybody laughed.

"The piece is known," he concluded lustily, "as 'Vladimir Tostoff's Jazz History of the World.' "

The nature of Mr. Tostoff's composition eluded me, because just as it began my eyes fell on Gatsby, standing alone on the marble steps and looking from one group to another with approving eyes. His tanned skin was drawn attractively tight on his face and his short hair looked as though it were trimmed every day. I could see nothing sinister about him. I wondered if the fact that he was not drinking helped to set him off from his guests, for it seemed to me that he grew more correct as the fraternal hilarity increased. When the "Jazz History of the World" was over girls were putting their heads on men's shoulders in a puppyish, convivial way, girls were swooning backward playfully into men's arms, even into groups, knowing that someone would arrest their falls—but no one swooned backward on Gatsby, and no French bob touched Gatsby's shoulder, and no singing quartets were formed with Gatsby's head for one link.

"I beg your pardon."

Gatsby's butler was suddenly standing beside us.

"Miss Baker?" he inquired, "I beg your pardon, but Mr. Gatsby would like to speak to you alone."

"With me?" she exclaimed in surprise.

"Yes, madame."

She got up slowly, raising her eyebrows at me in astonishment, and followed the butler toward the house. I noticed that she wore her evening-dress, all her dresses, like sports clothes—there was a jauntiness about her movements as if she had first learned to walk upon golf courses on clean, crisp mornings.

I was alone and it was almost two. For some time confused and intriguing sounds had issued from a long, many-windowed room which overhung the terrace.

The Marmon was manufactured in Indianapolis 1904-1933. This seven-passenger touring car was a 1930 offering.

Eluding Jordan's undergraduate, who was now engaged in an obstetrical conversation with two chorus girls, and who implored me to join him, I went inside.

The large room was full of people. One of the girls in yellow was playing the piano, and beside her stood a tall, red-haired young lady from a famous chorus, engaged in song. She had drunk a quantity of champagne, and during the course of her song she had decided, ineptly, that everything was very, very sad—she was not only singing, she was weeping too. Whenever there was a pause in the song she filled it with gasping, broken sobs, and then took up the lyric again in a quavering soprano. The tears coursed down her cheeks—not freely, however, for when they came into contact with her heavily beaded eyelashes they assumed an inky color, and pursued the rest of their way in slow black rivulets. A humorous suggestion was made that she sing the notes on her face, whereupon she threw up her hands, sank into a chair, and went off into a deep vinous sleep.

"She had a fight with a man who says he's her husband," explained a girl at my elbow.

I looked around. Most of the remaining women were now having fights with men said to be their husbands. Even Jordan's party, the quartet from East Egg, were rent asunder by dissension. One of the men was talking with curious intensity to a young actress, and his wife, after attempting to laugh at the situation in a dignified and indifferent way, broke down entirely and resorted to flank attacks—at intervals she appeared suddenly at his side like an angry diamond, and hissed: "You promised!" into his ear.

The reluctance to go home was not confined to wayward men. The hall was at present occupied by two deplorably sober men and their highly indignant wives. The wives were sympathizing with each other in slightly raised voices.

"Whenever he sees I'm having a good time he wants to go home."

"Never heard anything so selfish in my life."

"We're always the first ones to leave."

"So are we."

"Well, we're almost the last tonight," said one of the men sheepishly. "The orchestra left half an hour ago."

In spite of this wives' agreement that such malevolence was beyond credibility, the dispute ended in a short struggle, and both wives were lifted, kicking, into the night.

As I waited for my hat in the hall the door of the library opened and Jordan Baker and Gatsby came out together. He was saying some last word to her, but the eagerness in his manner tightened abruptly into formality as several people approached him to say good-bye.

Jordan's party were calling impa-

Fashions and fun from the '20s. On the opposite page, a 1922 Post *cover (skirts got shorter as the decade progressed). Here, a scene from* Our Modern Maidens, *a 1929 movie starring Joan Crawford. Fitzgerald himself praised Joan's characterization of the flapper who would shake her wind-blown bob and dance herself into a frenzy while the saxes shrieked and the trombones wailed, and then be ready for a midnight joyride.*

tiently to her from the porch, but she lingered for a moment to shake hands.

"I've just heard the most amazing thing," she whispered. "How long were we in there?"

"Why, about an hour."

"It was . . . simply amazing," she repeated abstractedly. "But I swore I wouldn't tell it and here I am tantalizing you." She yawned gracefully in my face. "Please come and see me. . . . Phone book . . . Under the name of Mrs. Sigourney Howard. . . . My aunt. . . ." She was hurrying off as she talked—her brown hand waved a jaunty salute as she melted into her party at the door.

Rather ashamed that on my first appearance I had stayed so late, I joined the last of Gatsby's guests, who were clustered around him. I wanted to explain that I'd hunted for him early in the evening and to apologize for not having known him in the garden.

"Don't mention it," he enjoined me eagerly. "Don't give it another thought, old sport." The familiar expression held no more familiarity than the hand which reassuringly brushed my shoulder. "And don't forget we're going up in the hydroplane tomorrow morning at nine o'clock."

Then the butler, behind his shoulder:

"Philadelphia wants you on the phone, sir."

"All right, in a minute. Tell them I'll be right there. . . . Good night."

"Good night."

"Good night." He smiled—and suddenly there

seemed to be a pleasant significance in having been among the last to go, as if he had desired it all the time. "Good night, old sport. . . . Good night."

But as I walked down the steps I saw that the evening was not quite over. Fifty feet from the door a dozen headlights illuminated a bizarre and tumultuous scene. In the ditch beside the road, right side up, but violently shorn of one wheel, rested a new coupé which had left Gatsby's drive not two minutes before. The sharp jut of a wall accounted for the detachment of the wheel, which was now getting considerable attention from half a dozen curious chauffeurs. However, as they had left their cars blocking the road, a harsh, discordant din from those in the rear had been audible for some time, and added to the already violent confusion of the scene.

A man in a long duster had dismounted from the wreck and now stood in the middle of the road, looking from the car to the tire and from the tire to the observers in a pleasant, puzzled way.

"See!" he explained. "It went in the ditch."

The fact was infinitely astonishing to him, and I recognized first the unusual quality of wonder, and then the man—it was the late patron of Gatsby's library.

"How'd it happen?"

He shrugged his shoulders.

"I know nothing whatever about mechanics," he said decisively.

"But how did it happen? Did you run into the wall?"

"Don't ask me," said Owl Eyes, washing his hands of the whole matter. "I know very little about driving—next to nothing. It happened, and that's all I know."

"Well, if you're a poor driver you oughtn't to try driving at night."

"But I wasn't even trying," he explained indignantly, "I wasn't even trying."

An awed hush fell upon the bystanders.

"Do you want to commit suicide?"

"You're lucky it was just a wheel! A bad driver and not even *try*ing!"

"You don't understand," explained the criminal. "I wasn't driving. There's another man in the car."

The shock that followed this declaration found voice in a sustained "Ah-h-h!" as the door of the coupé swung slowly open. The crowd—it was now a crowd—stepped back involuntarily, and when the door had opened wide there was a ghostly pause. Then, very gradually, part by part, a pale, dangling individual stepped out of the wreck, pawing tentatively at the ground with a large uncertain dancing shoe.

Blinded by the glare of the headlights and confused

Standing on the running board of a moving automobile was fun but dangerous and, in many places, against the law. Eliminating running boards doubtless saved thousands of lives over the years. The beach fashions and sporty Marmon shown here date from 1925. Books published that year included Sinclair Lewis's Arrowsmith *and Theodore Dreiser's* An American Tragedy *as well as* Gatsby. *The Florida land boom was on. Courtroom dramas played out that year included the court-martial of Colonel Billy Mitchell and the Scopes "monkey trial."*

By 1932 it was clear that the party was over. The stock-market slide of October, 1929, was only the beginning of the end. There was optimism early in 1931, but by the end of that year 3,000 banks had failed and 9 million workers were unemployed (one out of three in some areas). In 1932 the Lindbergh baby was kidnapped; Amelia Earhart flew the Atlantic; Franklin Roosevelt was elected President. Auto production was just one-fourth of what it had been in 1929 but there were still too many new cars, too few buyers. Shown here: a 1932 Packard.

by the incessant groaning of the horns, the apparition stood swaying for a moment before he perceived the man in the duster.

"Wha's matter?" he inquired calmly. "Did we run outa gas?"

"Look!"

Half a dozen fingers pointed at the amputated wheel—he stared at it for a moment, and then looked upward as though he suspected that it had dropped from the sky.

"It came off," someone explained.

He nodded.

"At first I din' notice we'd stopped."

A pause. Then, taking a long breath and straightening his shoulders, he remarked in a determined voice:

"Wonder'ff tell me where there's a gas'line station?"

At least a dozen men, some of them a little better off than he was, explained to him that wheel and car were no longer joined by any physical bond.

"Back out," he suggested after a moment. "Put her in reverse."

"But the *wheel's* off!"

He hesitated.

"No harm in trying," he said.

The caterwauling horns had reached a crescendo and I turned away and cut across the lawn toward home. I glanced back once. A wafer of a moon was shining over Gatsby's house, making the night fine as before, and surviving the laughter and the sound of his still glowing garden. A sudden emptiness seemed to flow now from the windows and the great doors, endowing with complete isolation the figure of the host, who stood on the porch, his hand up in a formal gesture of farewell.

(1925)

For the Fun of It

If the automobile became our workhorse and the magic carpet that carried us to adventure, it also became our toy. Little boys learned to lisp "ma-ma," "da-da" and then "car-car"; they went to sleep clutching toy trucks instead of teddy bears.

Over the years this toy of ours has been good for a lot of laughs. Auto humor began when the first passenger in a buggy leaned out and shouted, to a motorist tinkering with his stalled car, "Get a horse!" It may have known its finest hour with Jack Benny, on radio in the '40s and TV in the '50s. It took only a mention of Jack's Maxwell to send the studio audience into spasms of laughter. It is, therefore, appropriate to begin this section with a picture of Jack's car, the 1920 Maxwell.

Mr. Migg Enters the Motor Age

By Ogden Nash, 1934

MR. MIGG belongs to the unhappy generation that was psychologically squashed between the tailboard of the buggy and the acetylene headlights of the Pope Toledo. Children born five years earlier than he arrived with a curry comb in one hand and a bridle in the other; five years later, they wore goggles and were equipped with drivers' licenses. To the class of 1902 alone belongs the doubtful privilege of instinctively distrusting both the horse and the automobile.

People proud of their modernity spoke rudely of horses during Mr. Migg's childhood; they wondered how they had ever put up with horses; their skittishness, their viciousness, their sloth, their undependability; Mr. Migg received the ineradicable impression that a horse was a combination of tapeworm, tiger

Horse meets Master—
a 1915 cover painting.

and tornado. He was definitely off horses. Once in his youth he gave a horse an apple because a girl asked him to and stood over him till he did it. He thinks it was the bravest act of his life, for he expected to lose his arm at the elbow. True, he still has his arm, but only, he is convinced, because that horse at the moment was gorged with elbows.

On the other hand, the very people who were selling their horses down the river, trading in their whips for monkey wrenches and turning their stables into garages, planted in Mr. Migg's mind a leeriness of automobiles which it has taken many years to uproot. The conversation of the pioneer motorist was prideful, but it reeked of disaster. It seemed to Mr. Migg that automobiles were always breaking down or blowing up. Their petty triumphs paled before their magnificent catastrophes. Even as the golfer who has sunk a forty-footer for a seventy-nine is shouted down by the fellow who has missed a six-inch putt to break a hundred, so was the Odysseus who had covered fifteen miles without mishap borne under before the windy boasting of the Ajax who, after spending three hours changing a tire, had discovered a leak in his gasoline tank, and the nearest source of supply a converted blacksmith shop a day's march away.

Mr. Migg's parallel uncomplimentary opinions of horses and automobiles merged one day in Savannah when a frightened horse jumped into the tonneau of the family Stevens Duryea. There was room for a horse in a 1909 tonneau, but not for the wagonload of watermelons which this one wanted to bring along. No one was hurt, but Mr. Migg's mind was made up. If he had to go from one place to another, he thought, give him the good old choo-choos every time.

Years passed. Automotive engineers spent thousands of sleepless nights figuring out ways to make life easier for the motorist. Finally one automotive engineer said to another automotive engineer "I've got it"; and the other automotive engineer said "What?" and the first automotive engineer said "Let's fix it so the motorist can motor sitting down." Everybody thought that was a splendid idea, and wondered why no one had ever thought of it before. The first step was to move

Members of an earlier generation dealt confidently with the horse, while those who came later—like the man in this photo—were masters of the auto.

the gas tank out from under the front seat. There was some stiff opposition to this move, as many people complained that getting out and lifting up the front seat every ten gallons or so gave them a needed opportunity to recover hairpins, love letters, odd change, latch keys and other small objects which they had been wondering where they were for days. Public reaction, on the whole, however, was favorable, and the automotive engineers went ahead. Lights, for example. It used to take two people to turn the lights on. One to stand twisting the jigger on the acetylene tank on the running board, and another to stand with a lighted match by the headlights. It could be done by one man, but he had to be exceptionally fast on his feet. If he took too long to cover the ground between the tank and the headlights, he was likely to be blown into the livery stable when he applied the match. This elaborate process finally struck some automotive engineer as being highly inconvenient. He was probably a slow-moving man with sore

feet; at any rate, he corrected it, and the rest of us can now turn on the lights without first stopping the car.

The designers were overcoming Mr. Migg's prejudices one by one. When they fixed it so that you could start the engine without going out front and winding it up, he succumbed. Not enough to do anything about a car of his own—he wasn't morally or financially equal to that, as yet—but at least enough to be driven in other people's cars without grinding the enamel off his teeth and jabbing his fingernails into the palms of his hands. He even speculated timidly on the possibility of someday learning to drive. It took several years for this idea to blossom, but eventually, on entering college, he borrowed his roommate's car, somehow passed a Massachusetts driver's test, and three hours later, turning out to avoid a truck, drove rapidly into the side of the Odd Fellows' Hall in Portsmouth, Rhode Island. He left his roommate to cope with the Odd Fellows and took a train back to Boston.

I Want a Crank and Running Boards

Frederick C. Othman, 1946

THE BOYS IN THE BACK ROOMS of the automobile factories are designing the new models now for year after next. I do not care whether these motorcars have atomic engines, nineteen cylinders, just two big ones or run on maple syrup. They may have body panels of steel, activated cat fur, aluminum, spun glass, solidified milk, magnesium or homogenized chewing gum. As long as the materials are serviceable, I am broad-minded.

But these babies with the slide rules are drawing the blueprints for my next sedan, and by all the smashed fenders on Highway No. 1 I've got the right to tell 'em how I want it built. Lend an ear, engineers, and give me no sneers. This is a customer talking: We will start at the prow of my new automobile, and as we work back you will take notes respectfully. Directly beneath the radiator you will bore a hole. Into it you will fit a revolutionary postwar motorcar accessory which I have invented and which I call, for want of a better name, the crank. There is nothing complicated, gentlemen, about the crank. I am presuming that the 1948 two-door sedan will depend upon the storage battery to get started. The storage battery's all right when it is all right, but on cold mornings it is inclined to curl up with its old dance programs and dream. When this happens I can insert my amazing invention, the crank, into the hole, turn it by hand and get the engine started.

If it is not too much trouble—and even if it is—I want you designers to chop another hole in the top of the radiator, outside in the daylight, and place upon it a lid. We will call this the radiator cap. If you care to decorate it with a naked lady in silver, a leering faun or an early-Gothic gargoyle with wings, I shall not object. I realize that you fellows regard yourselves as artists who must express your own originality. My interest is in pouring water into my engine as the necessity arises without having to hire the crew of a tow car to help me open the hood. Come to think of it, my friends, let us also improve the hood.

We will throw away the self-locking machinery, the springs, the cables and the big knob on the dash. We will replace all this with small handles on either side of the hood, so that either side may be opened with a flick of the wrist.

Lift the hood now and inspect the widgets, gadgets and mysterious ganglia, with copper tubes leading therefrom, which you have installed for the last several years around automobile engines. These, you will regret to hear, have caused my bride already to doubt my infallibility. She believes—and I have every reason to believe she's right—that I am ignorant of their use. This I can tolerate no longer. You will kindly rip from my new automobile most of those small black boxes with the setscrews on their under surfaces; if you find any that are absolutely necessary to my travel, you will label them so that I, knowing what they are, will not be insulted more than necessary by my passenger.

The engine itself I leave to you experts. It may have helical gears or no gears; you may cut your initials, if you want, in the piston heads. All I want is for it to run after I get it started, and to keep on running until I, its master, turn off the ignition switch. . . .

Join me now, experts, on the front seat of my new automobile; on the soft front seat, let me add. This seat, if it will make your lives pleasanter, may be wide enough for sixteen acrobats and a spotted dog, but mostly I'll be sitting on it alone. I'd like to be comfortable. I know this is a revolutionary thought, but what I really want is a seat on which I can sit up straight with my knees no higher than my hips. It may be possible for you gentlemen to borrow a chair and copy its dimensions.

This seat must be one which I can reach without knocking off my hat, skinning my shins or ruining my shine. I know that I am presenting a whale of a problem, but I have given it serious thought and again I have a unique idea. Alfresco running boards!

I honestly do believe you designers have been on the right track. You have, indeed, installed within your recent vehicles strips of molding which are rudimentary running boards. What good are they when the doors are closed? Don't you fellows know that one of the pleasures of owning a motorcar should be parking it beneath a tree in the side yard on a

hot afternoon, sitting on the big, wide, outside-the-door running board and discussing politics, crops, ladies and atomic energy with the next-door neighbor? And how can you do that if the running boards are locked up inside? . . .

Let us consider frankly now a delicate subject. We must be brave, control our tendency to blush, and speak out. Just what, my friends, is indecent about an automobile tire: Why do you insist upon concealing it in enameled steel pantalets? Does it connote something you may have read in Havelock Ellis?

Perhaps I am a very vulgar fellow. It may be that I do not understand the niceties, but I am not ashamed of my tires. I want to see them uncovered in front of everybody, including my old mother, who is not so easily shocked as you might think. What I am leading up to, gentlemen, are my fenders. These will be designed solely for the purpose of keeping mud from being splashed on me. They will not resemble the pontoons of flying boats; neither will they bulge, nor flow down in sweeping

Late in the '40s cars began to look less like cars. The radiator, body and fenders lost their separate identities; all angles melted into curves. Shown here: Mercury and Lincoln for 1949.

The author of this selection would have liked the 1914 Overland with radiator cap, small fenders, and a running board for sitting on.

lines to stab me when I'm crawling under to get the jack beneath the axle. . . .

I must emphasize that these thoughts on improving the new models are not random ones. Neither are they capricious. I even consulted your local representative, the one in the greasy coveralls, name of Joe, who has spent the last seven years trying to keep my present heap among the running. He admitted my ideas had merit individually, but when considered collectively, what would they do to streamlining?

Gentlemen, please. I don't want a rocket to the moon, or a submarine, or a jet-propelled flying machine. I need an automobile with four wheels and a minimum of squeaks. It will travel on the earth without ever taking off, at a maximum speed of forty-five miles per hour.

Most people preferred progress. They were happy to trade crank for self-starter and running boards for enclosed trunk space at the rear.

If my inventions make this vehicle look a little square in spots, what is wrong with that?

Joe said, in fact, that the magnificent 1948 motorcar I have envisaged sounded to him like a 1918 model Velie Velvet Four. That indicates how far he is behind the times. What I actually had in mind was my father's 1920 Auburn Beauty Six. Sometimes in the country away from the danger of scarring the red varnish, he would let me drive it. There, gentlemen, was an automobile.

It even smelled good. This was because of the genuine leather upholstery, the hand-rubbed-walnut interior trimmings and the crystal vase in which my mother, in season, kept roses. This vase, as it happens, still is in our garage. It is a beauty. If it will help, I can ship it to Detroit, so that you engineers may build my dream car around it.

40 Memories to the Gallon

by Starkey Flythe, Jr., 1976

WE SAT ON THE PORCH, under the yellow bug light, until it got so hot my father said, "Let's take a ride." It meant more than his saying "I'm going to give each of you a million dollars." The dog thought so too. "Why do dogs want to go to ride, Pa?" "The same reason you do, son."

The car was a Packard, a good car, that was to last us for the "duration," that indeterminate block of time in which the war, Roosevelt and all the horrors of the world were disposed of. Most people longed more for a new car than for peace though.

There was no gasoline and there was a man down the street they said went to sea at night and met German submarines to swap food for gas and when he got home at night (late, presumably since we were 150 miles from the ocean) he would sell scrap metal to the Japanese. We knew all this because he had a new car.

The starvation effect of the duration without cars produced such a distortion of time that many of us still think, in terms of cars, that anything postwar is brand-new.

Granny had an old Graham Paige. It had shades inside on all the windows—except the front. She cherished (there is no other word) a notion that she was next. After McKinley that is. There was no sweeter, more docile soul than Granny. But somehow she thought they were out to get her. Of course, with all the blinds drawn, it was difficult to see, and looking at her fenders' (the Graham's) dents suggested she was missing a few things (visually, not factually).

The American mind is full of these bits and pieces. "I went out on my first date in a Nash Rambler." "I'll never forget; we were just married, I had a brand-new 1950 Pontiac."

There is the story of a man who invented something—some gadget which would go on every single car ever made, and after they paid him, they asked him what he wanted and he said a new 1949 Buick every year forever. And they kept the die just for him. And of course he never did die and somewhere in the streets of Chattanooga he's still tooling around in that '49 Buick.

A few lucky Americans were able to buy new cars like this 1947 Nash soon after the war ended; more waited and kept repairing their old cars. One way or another, everyone was on the road again by 1957 when Norman Rockwell painted the two scenes opposite.

Norman Rockwell

Suburbia through the eyes of Post cover artists. Above, trick-or-treaters pass before that symbol of affluence, the two-car garage. (By John Falter, 1958.) Opposite, frustration at the tollbooth, by Stevan Dohanos, 1956.

The Second-Car Ten-Day War

By Erma Bombeck

WE HAD TALKED about the isolation of the suburbs and the expense of a second car before moving there and I thought I had made my position very clear.

I did not want a car. Did not need a car. And would not take a car if it were offered me.

I lied.

"I've got to have wheels," I said to my husband one night after dinner.

"We've talked about this before," he said, "and we agreed that the reason we migrated was to explore all the adventures the suburbs have to offer."

"I've explored both of them. Now I need a car. A car will put me in touch with the outside world. It will be my link with another culture, another civilization, another world of trade."

"Aren't you being a little dramatic?" he suggested.

"Let me lay it on you, Cleavie, the high spot in my day is taking knots out of shoestrings—with my teeth—that a kid has wet on all day long. I'm beginning to have feelings for my shower-massage pik. Yesterday, I etched a dirty word on the leaf of my philodendron."

"And you think a car is going to help you?"

"Of course it will help. I'll be able to go to the store, join a bowling league, have lunch downtown with the girls, volunteer, go to the dentist, take long drives in the country. I want to see the big, outside world from atop a lube rack. I want to whirl dizzily in a cloud of exhaust, rotate my tires with the rest of the girls. Don't you understand? I want to *honk* if I love Jesus!"

For a reason I was soon to understand, *all* of us went to the showroom to pick out *my* car. Within minutes, I saw it. It was a bright, yellow sports number—a one-seater that puts you three inches off the ground and sounds like a volcano when the motor turns over. Near to ecstasy, I closed my eyes and imagined myself at a traffic light, my large sunglasses on top of my head like Marlo Thomas, and as I quickly brushed lip gloss on my lips from a small pot, a dark stranger from the car next to me shouted, "Could we meet and talk?" And I laughed cruelly, "Don't be a fool! I'm a homeroom mother!" and sped off.

The rest of the family was gathered around a four-wheel-drive station wagon with a spare tire on top, space for extra gas cans along the back and fold-down seats giving you room to transport the Cleveland Symphony and all their instruments.

"Hey, is this a car?" asked my husband, eyes shining.

"That was *my* next question," I said. "Look, I don't want transportation to a war, I just want a car to take me to the store and back."

Above, frustration in the no-passing lane, by Stevan Dohanos, 1954. Opposite, heartbreak at the boarding kennel, by Earl Mayan, 1957.

"Of course you do," he said, "and this is the no-nonsense car that can get the job done."

Oh, I tried all right to hide my disappointment. I put glasses on top of my head, touched up my lip gloss at traffic lights, and even occasionally ran my tongue over my lips like Jennifer O'Neill, but I never climbed behind the wheel of that orthopedic vehicle without feeling like I was following General Patton into Belgium.

Besides, I was the only woman in the neighborhood with a big wagon. All the others tooled around in small, sleek sports cars that had previously belonged to their husbands.

By the end of the first week, the newness of owning my own car had begun to wear off. I had transported six kids a day to school, a power mower to the repair shop, a porch swing for a garage sale, and the neighbor's dog to the vet who would not fit into a Volkswagen, Nova, Pontiac, Plymouth, Oldsmobile, Tank, or Global Van Lines.

The second week things picked up. I transported thirty-five sleeping bags and supplies for a week at camp, paneling from a lumber yard which wouldn't make delivery until the following week, a missile launch for a science fair, eight baseball bats, four base bags and twelve Little-League players, eight bags of fertilizer for the lawn and six surly homeroom mothers who arrived at a tea smelling like fertilizer.

It was of no comfort to me whatsoever knowing that I would make U-Haul Mother of the Year. I had to unload that car. Things came to a head one afternoon when I stopped for a traffic light and a huge transport truck pulled alongside me. The ones that travel all night to get your bread fresh to you in the morning. While waiting for the light to change, a burly driver looked over and shouted, "Hey, Mac, where's a good place to eat and get some sack time?"

I knew then I had to make my move and trade up—to my husband's car.

"You don't suppose we could switch cars?" I asked that night after dinner.

"Why would we want to do a thing like that?" he asked.

I hesitated dramatically, "I didn't want to tell you but the children get drowsy in the back seat. I think something is leaking in."

"Then, by all means, take it to the garage and have it fixed." (STRIKE ONE.)

"I'm in the garage so often now, I have my own key to the restroom. What would you say if I told you I only get seven miles to the gallon and I'm costing you $1.50 every time I wait for a light to turn green?"

"We knew the car would be an added expense when we bought it." (STRIKE TWO.)

"It's really a shame for your new, small, compact car to sit out all day in the harsh sun and the rain and the cold when it could sit in a nice, warm garage."

"There's something to that, but how would you transport all those children every day?" (BALL ONE.)

"I just read a survey that a smaller car is safer because the children are packed together and do not have room to swing around and argue about who gets a window."

"That makes sense (BALL TWO) but what would I do with a big car that eats gas and attracts burly truck drivers?" (BALL THREE.)

It was three and two and I wound up for the big one.

"In a way it's a shame you don't have the station wagon. That way you could pick up some paying riders who would love transportation to the city. The extra money would pay for your gas."

HOME RUN!

"It's funny you should mention that," he said. "The Osborns' daughter, Fluffy, asked me just the other day if I had room in my car for her to ride to the city."

"You mean the girl in the next block who always looks like she's wearing a life preserver?"

"What a thing to say. She just has good posture."

"That's inflatable—I mean debatable."

"Then it's settled. We trade cars. You can drive mine and I'll take the wagon."

I never knew victory could make you feel so rotten.

Car-toons

1922—1961

"See? Just push the button and down she go[es]"

"I hope you'll excuse the look of the place—George made a hard right turn."

Drive-in Movie

THE SATURDAY EVENING POST

"Would you mind waiting until the battle scene to drive in?"

MORT WALKER.

DRAWN BY GEORGE H. MABIE

"Calling Car Seventeen. . . . In-vestigate Auto Crash. . . . Car Seventeen. . . . Corner of North and Main"

"In a way I'm glad it happened—I prefer a small car."

"Well, shall we chance it?"

ROAD UNDER REPAIR
TRAVEL AT
YOUR OWN RISK

"A fine car you swiped for our getaway!"

"No. That isn't the cigarette lighter."

"Sure, Five Tickets! Five Passed the Red Light, Didn't They?"

DRAWN BY LAWRENCE LA RIAR

"Don't get out; I can hear you from th

"Mind if I stay here and watch awhile?"

DRAWN BY REAMER KEL

"Ed would have preferred a slamomatic car with a frabulated clutch or some silly thing—but I insisted I wanted a blue one."

THE SATURDAY EVENING POST

"Oh, Shut Up, You Nasty Cheerful Little Beast!"

"...on't Tell Me, Now! Let Me Find It"

MAC'S GARAGE

"You're the new man, I presume?"

THE SATURDAY EVENING POST

The Men
Who Made the
Motor Age

They were legion, the mechanically minded men who tinkered with wheels and engines in old stables and machine shops, in the early years of the century. There were fortunes to be made because, as William S. Knudson said, "Everybody wants to go from A to B sitting down." Almost overnight, a new industry was born, suffered growing pains, and became the American giant. Here, a 1929 Chevrolet casts a broad shadow on the land.

Duryea's first gasoline-powered vehicle, operated by him in 1892.

It Doesn't Pay to Pioneer

By Charles E. Duryea, 1931

IT IS MY BELIEF that I designed and built the first gasoline automobile actually to run in America, sold the first car on this side, did the first automobile advertising and won the first two American races. The last two claims cannot be disputed; the first two have been; though no one else offers proofs acceptable in court, as I do, of operation of a gasoline vehicle as early as April 19, 1892, or sales as early as the summer of 1896.

History is a none too dependable decider of such questions. The invention of the steamboat still is disputed after more than a century, and credit is popularly given to Robert Fulton, who no more invented it than Lindbergh did the airplane. Many men moved boats by steam before Fulton. It may even be that the twenty-first century will think of Henry Ford as the inventor of the automobile. A leader is not the man who first brings a cause to the fore, but the man who keeps it there. Until there are followers, there can be no leader.

I rest my case on the evidence, but while there is yet time I should like to read into the record the fact that most of the fundamentals of the motorcar were American-born, not European, and were demonstrated practicably a generation or more before the first horse ever bolted at the sight of a go-devil.

It doesn't pay to pioneer; not in money, at any rate. It's the early Christian, as Saki said, who gets the fattest lion. Like my brother and my fellow pioneers, Haynes and the Appersons, C. B. King and Alex Winton, my name no longer is borne by any car.

The name of our contemporary, R. E. Olds, is perpetuated in the Oldsmobile and the Reo, though he long ago surrendered his interest in the names. Like most of them, and the inventors of the airplane, I was a bicycle mechanic, and like all of them, a mechanic without technical training. There are other names that go much farther back, names that no one knows—Samuel Morey, Dr. C. G. Page, Thomas Davenport, S. Perry, W. M. Storm, Dr. A. Drake, G. B. Brayton and H. K. Shanck.

The essential elements of the modern automobile are a knuckled front axle, a multiple-cylinder, internal-combustion engine with balanced crank shaft, electric ignition, spray carburetor, throttle control coupled to a change of speed gears, transmitting power to two driving wheels through a differential, the wheels having air tires and antifriction bearings. The self-starter was not regarded as an essential until motors became much larger.

How did this engine arrive? Let us trace its course, keeping in mind that around its experimenters existed vacuum, steam and hot-air engines, but that none of these solved the problem satisfactorily. The two-cylinder, 180-degree-crank, internal-combustion engine with poppet valves, cam operated, using liquid fuel fired by a timed electric spark and vaporized in a heated carburetor—the world's first—was patented in the United States and Great Britain in 1826 and described in two scientific journals of that year. Samuel Morey, of New Hampshire, one of the many to operate

Duryea in the 1895 vehicle he called "America's first real automobile."

steamboats before Fulton, was the inventor. The fuel was turpentine, of which we had a large and cheap supply. Morey tried many experiments, and by using an electric spark was able to put a compressed-burned charge above the piston before it started downward.

A decade later, Thomas Davenport, of Vermont, gave the world the rotary armature now used in starter

The Stanley twins, Francis and Freeland, in their 1896 Stanley Steamer.

generators, and made with it a small locomotive which he showed both in New York and London.

The jump coil with its vibrator was made by Dr. C. G. Page, of Salem, Massachusetts, and described in a scientific publication in 1839, a dozen years before the commonly credited French inventor showed it.

Go far enough back and you will find Franklin, in 1749, firing a spoonful of spirit on the opposite bank of the Schuylkill River with an electric spark to prove that electricity could be transmitted by wire. A Professor Hare, of the University of Pennsylvania, anticipated the incandescent electric lamp in the 1820's, using a platinum wire in nitrogen gas in an inverted drinking glass, sealed in water. Priority in invention often is a baffling thing to trace.

S. Perry, of Newport, New York, patented air and water cooled internal-combustion engines in 1843, exhibited and advertised them in New York, equipped them with self-starters in 1846. In 1851, W. M. Storm, of New York City, patented an engine which compressed the air used before ignition and employed a jump

spark with engine-driven dynamo for supplying the current. He gave us modern compression a quarter of a century before Otto copied the Frenchman, De Rochas.

Doctor Drake's exhibition at the Crystal Palace, New York, followed closely in 1855, showing an engine which he advocated for locomotive use and for "vessels even to China," because of its compact liquid fuel. Advertised in the *Scientific American* and patented abroad, it was known to Lenoir, who made several like it, using gas fuel, half a dozen years later.

George B. Brayton, of Rhode Island, appeared in 1852 and devoted the next forty years of his life to the gas engine, of which he is the real father, and had constantly in mind its application to horseless carriages. He gave us a new cycle of operation that ran with the certainty and sweetness of a steam engine and was related to the Diesel of recent years. One of his gasoline engines was fitted to a Providence street car in 1873 and another to a Pittsburgh omnibus in 1878, but both were denied the streets. In January, 1876, he licensed Joshua Rose and A. R. Shattuck, both men of prominence, to make road motor vehicles.

Two Brayton gas engines pumped air for the Aquarium at the Philadelphia Centennial while Otto still was showing free-piston engines in which the charge shot the piston into the air, and gravity and air pressure on the downward stroke drove the flywheel. "The Brayton engine looked and ran like a sweetly designed steam engine, while the Otto was anything

George B. Seldon in the 1877 vehicle he called "America's first car."

else," said the *Scientific American*'s Centennial report. Otto promptly brought out his "silent," which, because of its greater economy, won shop favor over the Brayton. David was not permitted to build the temple, and Brayton died in 1892 without having seen the adoption of the horseless carriage he envisaged.

In 1883, H. K. Shanck was a tricycle maker at Dayton, Ohio, and began to apply gas-engine power to his machines. I saw his engine at the Ohio State Fair in 1886, the first combination of the electric spark, carburetor and liquid fuel in my experience. I recognized in it the key to the age-old problems of flight and self-propulsion, and in the next decade worked out and published a practical solution of human flight and made and proved the essentials of the successful motor vehicle.

The knuckled front axle was shown in 1818 and accredited to Akerman, of England. The differential was shown by Pecqueer, of France, in 1828. Goodyear, the American, vulcanized rubber in 1839, and Thompson, the Englishman, applied the discovery to air tires six years later. Devices for varying speed were common to many machines.

The early carburetors were not well adapted to varying speeds or volume of charge, and the spray carburetor and throttle control for automobiles are believed to have been used first on a Duryea. My wife's perfume atomizer suggested the spray carburetor to me, shortly after I had seen Shanck's Morey device. A Duryea car made in 1894-95 was the first to use pneumatic tires, though they already were general on bicycles. The bicycle already had ball bearings.

Why was it, with the fundamentals of both the motorcar and the airplane already solved, that their appearance was so long delayed? And why was the solution waived by organized industry and engineers to obscure mechanics without technical training?

Because of the weight of a unanimous and intolerant public opinion that both ideas were too silly for words, one as silly as the other—an opinion so stubbornly held that it rejected the testimony of its own eyes. In 1895, when I invited Samuel Bowles II, famous editor of the Springfield *Republican*, to ride in the Duryea which won the first American automobile race, his reply was: "I appreciate your kindness, but really, it would not be compatible with my position." The automobile was an absurdity, wherefore it was ridiculous to be seen in one.

Graduate engineers knew that flying and road transport of small vehicles were the two oldest and toughest nuts of mechanics. They knew the answers had been sought endlessly to virtually no practical result. And they were practical men, busy as trained technicians are likely to be, with routine jobs for which a demand existed.

It is a mistake to suppose that either the automobile or the airplane was created to supply a demand. The demand was very painfully built up after the machines had been proved, and many of the pioneers foundered.

The reasons are three why America was destined to be the home of the automobile—great distances, scarce labor and cheap fuel. It is surprising only that the automobile was so long delayed. It was partly chance that the steam auto did not appear coincidently with the steam train. The obvious ideal of mechanical locomotion was the greatest possible freedom of movement, but when Stephenson invented his steam locomotive, it was crudely heavy, while the public roads were bad. So railroads were built especially for the locomotive. In that way the cart got before the horse. Instead of simplifying and lightening the locomotive, it was made heavier and heavier and more and more restricted to rails and a private right of way. That in turn fixed in the public mind the fallacy that no mechanically propelled vehicle belonged on the highway.

Hundreds of forgotten men, however, did operate steam road vehicles of one kind or another in the century before the automobile age dawned. Nothing came of it because of public hostility. When the automobile era finally opened, the gas car, though it led easily in performance, was the Cinderella of the trade. The electric marvels of the trolley car, the telephone and the Edison lamp had captured the public imagination. Down to 1900—even later—one of the greatest sales obstacles the gasoline car had to overcome was the general conviction that any day Edison would invent a miraculous auto that would sweep the market. Next to

Electric taxicabs of 1896 looked like horseless hansom cabs.

This 1904 runabout preserved the curves of the horse-drawn victoria.

the electric came the steam car, because of public familiarity with steam and its fifty years' advantage in engineering practice. Steam ran the railroads, electricity the trolley cars, while the internal-combustion engine was unknown to the layman.

To the Chicago World's Fair, in my opinion, belongs first credit for the automobile. Just as the Philadelphia Centennial sponsored the bicycle, Chicago stood godmother to the motorcar. An English high-wheel bicycle and a French steam velocipede exhibited at the Centennial in 1876 set off the bicycle craze. The Chicago Fair in 1890 and 1891 advertised throughout the world in many languages for exhibits, offering awards. One class was for "steam, electric and other road vehicles propelled by other than animal power." Note the absence of any specific mention of the internal-combustion engine.

This at once put the problem in a new light, gave it needed dignity and prestige. A thousand experimenters who had been discouraged by ridicule and pity took a fresh hitch at their trousers. I was one of these. What we were able to produce by 1893 was pitifully meager, but 1894 brought enough cars to permit a race in France,

won by a steamer, and the next year the first American race was run at Chicago. My third car, begun late in 1893, won that race and a $2000 prize over Europe's three entries. It was, in my judgment, the first true automobile, combining all modern essentials for the first time. Four Duryeas won all prizes, totaling $3000, in the second American race on Memorial Day, 1896. The same year two Duryeas won the first British road race, London to Brighton, against the best foreign cars.

It doesn't pay to pioneer, and yet the first American investor to put money into an automobile venture got his capital back with a profit. He was Edwin F. Markham, a nurse, of Springfield, Massachusetts. I was canvassing for funds to build our first model. Banks were out of the question, of course. The tobacconists of Springfield seemed to be prosperous and I was concentrating on them this day in the early '90s. Markham, lounging in one shop, overheard my sales talk. In return for a tenth interest, he agreed to pay bills up to $1000. If he financed us to a self-supporting basis, he was to get a half interest. Eventually he put up $3000 and got back about $5000. He lived to see the automobile a commonplace and was very proud of his vision.

Henry Ford's first car was completed in 1896. His wife Clara kept him company evenings while he tinkered in the shed behind their Detroit home.

Henry Ford and His Men

Anonymous, 1926

NOT THE LEAST of Henry Ford's success has been due to his broad democracy of spirit. He's at home with anyone and intensely human with all. He tells some very amusing stories on himself. One day he was driving through the countryside in a flivver. He has many large, powerful and fashionable cars, but he often toots off in his faithful lizzie like an old-time prince, incognito. On a deserted roadside he found a big handsome touring car stalled, well-dressed ladies in the plush back seat, and a gentleman swearing not too softly under the upraised hood. Mr. Ford summarily halted lizzie, got out and politely asked if there was anything he could do to help. The man lifted his freshly begreased hands with an air of despair and pointed to the mute engine. Ford tinkered a minute—only a slight adjustment was needed—and the motor purred off like a newly awakened kitten. The man opened his wallet and handed a dollar bill toward Mr. Ford, who waved it back.

"Go on, it's worth more than that to have that blamed thing fixed."

Mr. Ford refused again.

"Why won't you take it?"

"Got too much money now," he said laconically as he got back into his namesake car.

"What! Too much money and riding around in a flivver!"

Mr. Ford smiled and drove on. The man never did learn who he was.

He's doing that sort of thing right along. Another time he was out riding in lizzie again and stopped to pick up a bum who was walking along the roadside. They got talking, and Ford sized the man up as a thorough vagabond, yet with something of good behind it all.

"Think I can get you a job when we get to Detroit." So without telling who he was, Ford led the fellow into his personnel department and had him hired with explicit instructions that if Bill wanted to leave he personally must be told about it. Bill soon learned that his erstwhile friend of the road was none other than the big boss of one of the greatest factories of the world, for he saw Mr. Ford from time to time around the plant. About spring the soles of Bill's feet began to itch for the dusty highways. He came to his immediate boss and said he had to leave; he had a sister in Montana who was very sick and he must see that she was properly taken care of. The boss retailed this to Mr. Ford, who made answer:

"Go back and tell Bill that we will wire to engage a trained nurse and the best doctors that can be got to take care of his sister."

That held Bill for a week, when he returned and said it wouldn't do because his sister wanted to see him and he had to go.

"Tell Bill," Mr. Ford replied, "that I will hire a special car with nurses and doctors to bring his sister here to Detroit so that he can be near her." And he would do it too!

Bill lasted another week; then he came back and said it was no use, his sister just wouldn't consent to it, he'd have to go to her. At this stage Mr. Ford went to see Bill himself.

"Bill, if you leave, I'll spend all my money having you trailed and have you locked up for vagabondage in every town you hit. Now look me straight in the eye. You haven't got a sister, have you?"

"No," confessed Bill.

"I thought maybe you hadn't, but if you had, I'd have done everything I said. It's nothing but the hobo in you coming back. Get busy and break up this wanderlust and make a man of yourself."

Today Bill is married, has two mighty fine children and a mighty good job. Small wonder there is loyalty, respect and industry in the Ford factory. No man can greatly succeed who does not like and understand men, whether these be his fellow men or his own workmen, for man is the motive power of all business.

Two views of early Ford assembly lines, and four versions of the 1914 Model T. Always black, the no-frills car nicknamed "tin lizzie" or "the flivver" was manufactured 1909-1927.

"See how these things all hang together. You cannot lower prices unless you improve methods. Improved methods can only work on the best of materials—poor materials are the most wasteful and expensive to work with—so the basic quality of your goods must improve. Economy requires that the very best labor be employed, and this calls for the highest wage—a cheap wage is always the dearest to everyone concerned, society most of all. It is strange that with all these values going up, prices can come down, but that is precisely the way it works. As prices come down to touch level after

level of purchasing power, production goes up. And as a general and far-flung result, the standard of wealth and purchasing power of the whole community rises."
—Henry Ford, 1936

The system worked for Mr. Ford. In 1914, when he raised the minimum daily wage of his assembly plant workers from $2.50 to $5, the cheapest Model T was priced at $825. By 1919 the price had been cut to $360, while production, sales and profits soared.

Boom before bust. In 1929 the auto industry turned out 4.5 million cars, but it was 20 long years before that record was broken. Shown here, some of the cars sold just before buyers disappeared from dealers' showrooms. On the opposite page, a 1930 Lincoln and 1929 Model A Ford with convertible tops raised and lowered by hand rather than by pushing a button on the dashboard. Here, the 1929 Ford convertible with top down, the 1928 Model A Ford sedan, and a 1932 Lincoln sedan with slanted windshield that hints at styling changes to come.

For 1936, new lines, a new kind of engine, and a new convenience feature—the trunk. Above, the Ford V-8 convertible sedan. If you could raise the down payment, you could buy this or any other Ford V-8 for $25 a month on a 1/2-percent-per-month finance plan. Below, the Lincoln-Zephyr V-12, a Ford car for the medium-price market.

Twenty years after the events described here Chrysler became head of the company that produced this handsome 1927 Dodge.

How I Learned to Drive

By Walter P. Chrysler, 1937

It was love at first sight when 33-year-old Chrysler laid eyes on the 1908 Locomobile touring car displayed at the Chicago Automobile Show. A railroad executive living in Iowa and earning $350 a month, Chrysler was hardly in position to own this "rich man's toy," but he bought it anyway. Friendly bankers who shared his faith in the infant automobile industry lent him the $4,300 he needed. The knowledge Chrysler gained tinkering with the Locomobile proved useful—he went on to become manager and then president of Buick Motor Co. and to found the corporation that still bears his name.

THE BARN in the backyard of our house in Oelwein was where we stored our garden tools, but more than half its space was cluttered with a lot of useless truck that had been left there by the former tenants of the premises. I began to clear this rubbish away, putting into a bonfire a dished buggy wheel, some dried-out, broken pieces of harness and bottles that had contained horse liniment. On that fire I dumped wheelbarrow loads of dust, straw and other litter, and did not stop until the barn was spick-and-span. By that time, my wife was excited by curiosity.

"I'm going to use it for a workshop."

"What are you going to make, dad?"

"Della, I've bought an automobile."

I told her all about it—that I had spent our cash reserve and gone in hock for more money than I would make in a year. She did not scold me, but it did seem to me that when she closed the kitchen door, it made a little more noise than usual; maybe she slammed it.

The automobile arrived in a freight car, anchored to the floor. I did not know how to run it, but I certainly was not going to allow another person to be the first behind its wheel. I arranged with a teamster to haul it to my house and put it in the barn. I cannot remember that I have ever been more jubilant than when Della, with Bernice in her arms and Thelma jumping up and down with excitement, saw me steer that horse-drawn car into the yard. If it had been a jewel of fantastic size, I could not have been more careful of it.

My wife was wild with enthusiasm then and wanted to take a ride immediately. But I put the car in the barn, and it stayed in there so long that she despaired of ever getting a ride. Sometimes she sat in it when I cranked up and let the engine run.

Night after night, I worked in the barn until it was time to go to bed, and some nights I did not leave the automobile until it was long past my bedtime. Saturday afternoons and all day on Sundays I worked on that car. I read automobile catalogues, I studied sketches and made still other sketches of my own. Most of the time, the innards were spread upon newspapers on the barn floor. There was no single function I did not study over and over. Finally, I proved to myself that I knew and understood it, because I had put it all together, had the engine tuned so that it was running like a watch.

"What is the use of having an automobile if we're never going to ride, dad?"

"Now, don't be impatient, Della."

"Impatient! You've had the car three months and it's never been out of the barn."

It was a Saturday afternoon, and so hot that I had taken off my coat and had my sleeves rolled up. I

Plymouth, new in 1928, was the Chrysler Corporation's entry in the low-priced field. This 1932 coupe with rumble seat sold for $610.

finished eating. "In the barn three months, you say? Well, this afternoon she's coming out. Come look!"

By then the noise of the Chryslers' Locomobile engine was a commonplace in our neighborhood, but somehow the word was quickly spread that this was an exceptional occasion. I had a gallery of neighbors, as I cranked up, got behind the wheel, one hand devoted to steering and one to fiddling with that confounded sliding transmission lever. In those days, the steering mechanism was still being placed on the right side. She had a chain drive, of course, and that was what made her seem to growl and snarl every time I touched the transmission lever. I swear, you would have thought the car was ticklish, the way she winced, but the engine was purring, and when I looked behind, I could see that she was not smoking, much. Then I clamped my teeth on a fresh cigar and engaged the clutch.

The big touring car bucked like a mustang saddled for the first time. We shot forward; as some of the neighbors whooped and yelled, she bucked again and lurched into a ditch, rolled half a length farther and stalled, axle deep, in my neighbor's garden patch.

I had chewed up about one third of my cigar on that short run. I sent off for a man who had a team of horses. He came, the trace chains clinking against the stones in the road. The fetlocks of his horses were caked with mud.

"Careful where you hook those chains! Mind that paint! Be careful! Want to ruin that car?"

"Say, mister, I've hauled cars before and will again. Keep your shirt on. I'll hold these horses."

We pulled her out; I settled with the teamster and promised monetary satisfaction to my irate neighbor. I heard a few mocking laughs, and so I cranked her up, jumped in behind the throbbing wheel and started off. This time I got her into high and let her roll. All I was doing was to grip the wheel and steer. I had to turn at

The Chrysler, new in 1928, offered the first high-compression engine, four-wheel brakes, balloon tires. Price of this 1931 sedan: $1,565.

the corner, but rather than make those chains growl and clash, I let her go in high. I won't swear that only two wheels were touching the ground, but I want to testify that it felt that way. As we leveled off, we were at the edge of Oelwein, right in the country.

Young Walt Chrysler, about the time he fell in love with cars.

A few hundred yards ahead, I saw a cow emerging from behind an osage hedge that bordered a lane. She was headed for the road. I bulbed the horn until it had made its gooselike cry four or five times, but the cow, a poor rack of bones draped with yellow hide, kept right on her course and never changed her pace; nor did I change the pace of the automobile. I could not; all that I could do was to grip the wheel and steer, biting on my cigar until my teeth met inside of it.

Well, I missed the cow, though I was close enough to touch her. I missed few of the ruts and holes along that country road to the section line where there was an intersecting road, and there I turned again—a little slower on this turn—and rode another mile before turning onto the third side of a quadrangular course that I knew would bring me home. I fed more gas to the four-cylinder engine on the street that led toward home. On the basis of ratings today, that car would be said to have about eighty horsepower. As I came up the grade, the neighbors saw me riding fast, maybe twenty miles an hour. I stopped at the barn. My neighbors helped me push the car inside. I closed the doors and then discovered I was so tired I trembled. There was not a dry stitch of clothing on me; that perspiration came from nervousness and excitement. It was six o'clock in the evening then. I went into the house, stripped off my clothes, took a bath and got into bed. I was all in from that wild ride. Well, that's the way I learned to drive. . . .

Inventor Kettering in action, 1911.

Boss Kettering and the Self-Starter

By Paul de Kruif, 1933

They called Charles F. Kettering a "monkey wrench scientist"—he was an inventor who worked side by side with his men at the struggling little Dayton Engineering Laboratories Company, housed in an Ohio barn. Henry Leland, president of the Cadillac Motor Company, was convinced

that "Ket" was the genius who could find a way to use a weak little electric storage battery to start a heavy automobile engine; he was so confident that he announced a "self-starter" would be available as optional equipment on his 1912 cars. Other people were less optimistic, though all agreed that the development of a better starter would enormously increase sales. Starting a car by cranking it was back-breaking, bone-shattering work. A good friend of Leland's had actually been killed when a whirling crank struck his jaw. Kettering did solve the mechanical problems involved. He went on to become a vice-president of General Motors; his little factory became Delco Products Division of GM.

THE CARDS were stacked against the Boss and his barn helpers. The probability of really inventing the self-starter varied inversely as the idea of having it was lovely. It wasn't only the professors and the experts who pooh-poohed it as being about as chimerical as perpetual motion. Boss Ket actually had to sell the electrical salesmen the idea of selling him goods, without which the self-starter could never have become a reality.

So now, this late, hot summer, while the boys in the barn were winding their coils, playing "When You and I Were Young, Maggie," on their battered phonograph, blotting the sweat off their drawings of unheard-of electric circuits, Boss Ket sat waiting and profoundly wool-gathering in his ridiculous little office. The cap he was wearing was cheap and greasy. His clothes did not become a general manager. He sat down on the small of his back. His long legs let him cock his big feet up on the very top of his rolltop desk in a way not seemly for any vice-president, even of so funny a little company as his own.

A stranger—young, snappy and natty—appeared in the doorway, stared, wabbled, and started to back out. "Hi, there," drawled the high-pitched voice of Kettering.

"I was looking for the Dayton Engineering Laboratories Company—for Mr. Kettering."

"Well?"

"You're not Mr. Charles F. Kettering?"

"Yeah."

Confusion fought with surprise on that young stranger's face. "My name's O. L. Harrison, and I've come——"

"Oh-h, so you're the fella that wants to sell us those storage batteries?"

On Mr. Harrison's face annoyance fought with pity.

"I may sell storage batteries. But I haven't come here to sell them."

Kettering hadn't budged, but looked owlishly at Harrison. "Yeah?"

"No, I've come all the way down from Cleveland to see just exactly what a man looks like who's crazy enough to want to order fifteen thousand of them," said the natty young man.

"Well, sit down, sit down. Let's talk it over," said the Boss, and in his voice there was no trace of offended vanity. . . .

Here and on the following pages, a family album of General Motors cars from the boom and bust years. First, the prestige cars with their elongated hoods and gleaming wire wheels. Opposite, a sporty 1927 Cadillac roadster. Right, the 1931 LaSalle. Below, the 1930 Cadillac V-16.

More conservative General Motors cars for middle-of-the-road, mid-price-range buyers. Above, the 1930 Pontiac sedan priced at $745, including the distinctive radiator ornament. (It was easy to identify makes then—everyone knew that the Indian's head meant Pontiac; the leaping ram, Dodge; the greyhound, Lincoln; the sailing ship, Plymouth.) Below and opposite, Oldsmobiles for 1929 and 1930 priced from $875 (for the coupe). Oldsmobile was—and is—the oldest name on the road. R. E. Olds produced and sold the first Oldsmobiles in 1901; he also made the Reo, which got its name from his initials.

General Motors had something for everyone. Above, a 1928 Buick for the young at heart; the other cars are Chevrolets for buyers with slender purses. The green two-door sedan is a 1928 Chevrolet priced at $585. (It was in 1928 that Chevrolet first outsold Ford, even though the Fords bore lower price tags. Third-best seller in the low price field: the Willys Whippet.) The black roadster is a 1931 Chevy, and the rainbow assortment of semi-streamlined cars are 1936 models.

The Auto in Our Lives

If the automobile gave to America new rituals of courtship—as in this 1920 Maxwell—it has also given us new kinds of housing, crime, eating habits, new heroes and new villains, a new initiation rite for the youth approaching adulthood—getting a driver's license—new solutions to old problems, and new problems for which we have not yet found solutions. On the following pages, Americans prominent in national affairs in the '60s share their thoughts about life with wheels.

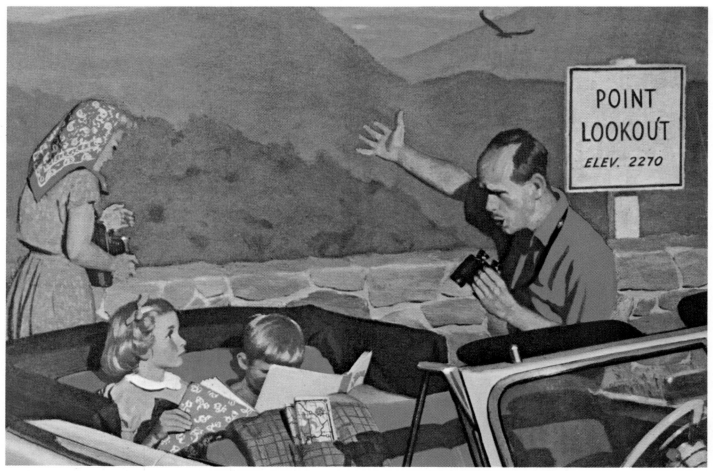

The family and the family car—three views by Post *cover artists. Above, hierarchical family structure preserved. (1953)*

Home is Where the Car is

Collected by W. H. Manville, 1968

GEORGE C. SCOTT, *highly acclaimed for his role in the Broadway hit,* Plaza Suite, *was seated on a blue sofa on the stage of the Plymouth Theater when I came to see him. He had just finished a matinée performance, and we looked out over the empty house while he talked about the family car providing a diagram of the American family:*

I'VE NOTICED that—troubled times or good times—some of our best times are when we're in our car. The car puts us all into roles; it is almost a diagram of the family we grew up thinking existed—but, which we found when we were grown, rarely does. As such, the car is almost a map of the ideal family which a child might draw.

Father is in the driver's seat. He is in control, responsible for the family's comfort and safety, and competent. He likes to drive. Mother is seated beside Father. She is equal to him, on a par with him—but she is not identical to him. She trusts him and his skill, and so

while he drives, she has time to turn to the back seat and tell the children to stop bouncing up and down and obstructing Father's view in the rearview mirror. I've noticed that Colleen, who is ordinarily very talkative and chatty, quiets down when we are driving somewhere. She handles the children, but still has a chance to sink back into herself, to think, to contemplate, to go back inside to what she is—rather than having to maintain a surface screen of nervous talk. Having me drive quiets some anxiety of her own.

The two boys are six and seven. That's them, in the back seat. They feel lively and peppy, because Father is driving. They have no responsibility, they are not being asked to grow up too soon. They jump and bounce around back there, but when Father tells them to quiet down, they do. Instinctively they seem to know that the price of their carefree irresponsibility is to listen to the man who is responsible—Father.

It's all a fantasy. People don't live this way anymore. It's like the national myth that we were all born on a farm or a small town, before we came to the city. This kind of hierarchical family structure doesn't go anymore—except for those few hours when we are all in the family car.

Teenage sons as auto experts. (By Amos Sewell, 1956)

WILLIAM BERNBACH *is chairman of the board of an advertising agency which has become famous on (and off) Madison Avenue for, among other things, its highly imaginative promotion of automobiles. Mr. Bernbach was recently asked how the average family decides on which car to buy.*

FATHER AND MOTHER want a car to take them where they want to go. Smoothly, comfortably, safely, of course—but their interest in cars just about ends there. And so when it's time to decide on which new car to buy, they turn to someone whose interest in cars goes much deeper. Someone who is a reader of *Road and Track*, for instance, who thinks about cars, compares them in his mind, knows all about engine performance, gasoline mileage and the difference between one model and another of the same brand name. He is the one who makes the decision, very often.

He's their teenage son.

MRS. WILLIAM RICHARDSON *lives in a beautiful town in Connecticut, and her husband commutes every day to his business in New York City. The Richardsons have a handsome house and three fine children, and Mrs. Richardson often spends more of her waking hours in her car than at home. Here she tells why.*

MY THREE CHILDREN all have different hours of going to school and returning. In addition, they all have their extracurricular activities: horseback riding for one, ballet for another, swimming classes for a third. And don't forget things like dentists, eye doctors, orthodontists, etc. And then there are trips to the supermarket, the laundry, the cobbler, the dry cleaner, and to take care of the list your husband has left you called "things to do today."

We're not still in the era when there was always a grandmother, a maiden aunt or some relative living in the house with you, and we certainly don't live in the age of servants, God knows. So when one child is home—mine are all young—and you have to go pick up another to ferry from here to there, you have to take the first one along. Of course, I have a baby-sitter whom I trust and use on occasion. But she doesn't drive, and so if I wanted her to sit with one child while I went to fetch another, first I'd have to take my child with me in the car to go get the baby-sitter, who would then sit with that child while I got the second one, and meanwhile the third one waits to go from school to his swimming class, and then I'd have to pack all the children in the car to take with me while I drove the baby-sitter home, and then stopped at the station to pick Bill up, and his train would be late, of course, and it all would be madness. So I skip the sitter.

A neighbor of mine points out that when my children get a little older—as hers are—they will have even more activities, and she says I'm not into this chauffeuring

Mother as chauffeur. (Sewell, again, 1960)

thing for real yet. My neighbor belongs to a mere twenty-three car pools a week.

Some families I know have to keep enormous charts to keep track of who will pick up whom, and where, and when, while other members of various car pools pick up someone else, someplace else, at some other time. If I had my choice of anyone in the world to have for help, it would be a chauffeur.

What makes me laugh is when I see wives at the station picking up their husbands who have just made the commute back from the city (you're used to his train being late, and maybe he's missed one, so you always keep a selection of books and magazines to read in the car). The wife slides over for "the better driver!" She's probably put in two hundred or two hundred fifty miles of driving that week—without ever leaving town. He's maybe driven ten that week—to the club for some golf, on Saturday.

F. LEE BAILEY, *the celebrated attorney, has fought murder charges against Dr. Sam Sheppard and Dr. Carl Coppolino. I asked him if he has had any brushes with the law himself:*

A COUPLE OF YEARS AGO I was feeling pretty good about the way my life was going, and I celebrated with a new car. A big Imperial, with a built-in desk, a work lamp and telephone—it even had a front seat that swiveled around so you could talk to the people in the back comfortably. The car was to be delivered New Year's Eve day.

I was out of town that day, and my wife picked me up at the airport when I flew in; she was in the new car. We were going off to Cape Cod to celebrate New Year's Eve—the plan was to drive directly there, right from the airport. (My wife had already packed my bags, and they were in the car.)

So off we went, my wife at the wheel, driving along at a pretty good clip. That's the way she drives. She's always aware of the speed limits, but goes along good.

Well, pretty soon I said to my wife, "Better slow down, I see a Blue Gumball Machine"; that's what we call our highway-patrol cars.

Well, he pulled us over to the side of the road anyway, and asked to see my wife's license. The way the breaks went, she'd just lost it the other day at the skating rink. So she said she didn't have it. Then he asked her for the car registration. In Massachusetts you have 48 hours to get a new car registration, and again, the breaks were, we didn't have ours yet on this brand-new car.

I realized it was all getting to look a little funny, so I got out of the car to talk to the officer. The police are part of my world, and I know many of them personally. Sure enough, I did know him, and he recognized me. I spoke to him a moment or two and told him that everything was really all right. So he backed off. But just as he turned away, he said something under his breath. I couldn't catch it, but it had an edge to it, so I asked him to repeat it. "Next time," he said, in a voice only I could hear, "bring your own wife."

I never laughed so hard in my life. You know why he thought my wife wouldn't show her license or registra-

Highway perils and problems—two views by Norman Rockwell. On the opposite page, the small-town speed trap (1929). Above, one more version of a favorite theme of magazine cover artists through the years. (1946).

tion? Because he thought she wasn't really my wife at all.

And you know who laughed at the story even harder than I did? My wife.

JOAN RIVERS, *the nightclub comedienne, tells this story about her first car—a secondhand wreck which a dealer had bartered to Joan's father (a doctor) in return for having saved his wife's life.* "He had never forgotten my father for that," *Joan says,* "nor forgiven him."

MY FATHER AND I always had fights about me borrowing the family car to go out and play my nightclub appearances. Boys think they have difficulties with their parents in borrowing the car to go out on dates. How about a girl who wants to borrow it to pursue a career her family disapproves of? Withholding transportation is a way that a lot of suburban families have of trying to control their kids' behavior; that way they don't have to say that what they really want to stop is whatever it is that the kid is going to do when he gets there. It's a parental device to win some silent, generational fight—but without arguing about the real issues.

Raymond Loewy designed the 1939 Studebaker, in appearance typical of the cars Americans were buying just before World War II. Americans went on driving cars that looked like this, when they could get gasoline for them, throughout the war years and until manufacturers retooled for new models in the late '40s. The Studebaker was manufactured in South Bend, 1902-1963.

But anyway, in the end, my father *did* give me this car, and I loved it. It only let me down once. I was on my way to one of my first nightclub dates. Besides the car, I had only one other possession in the world—my wig, which I used in my act. It made me beautiful, and I'd kiss it when I took it off; I used to call it little Joan, it meant so much to me. On this one night, the car let me down. It stopped right on a busy highway. I ran out, looking for help, taking the wig with me, of course. "Help me! Help me!" I shouted. Finally, I held the wig out as a kind of distress flag—it was ash blonde and gleamed. But I dropped it, and a car ran over it. I was in tears. Because it had cost me $125, and now it said "Firestone." The other car screeched to a halt, and the worried driver ran back to where I was. "Oh, lady, I'm sorry," he said. "I killed your dog."

MRS. SCOTT CARPENTER, *wife of the astronaut, has achieved a good measure of recognition herself as a newspaper columnist who has been syndicated in over 100 papers. I asked her what it was like to drive with a man who is used to whirling around the earth at 18,000 mph.*

WHEN SCOTT DRIVES, he brings his space-capsule thinking to the situation. He never wants to stop, and he never wants to slow down. He wants the car to be as self-contained and as fully controlled as possible. When we bought our last family car—we have four children,

so it's a station wagon—he asked Detroit to make so many modifications in the control system that they wired back, "Do you want to drive this car, or launch it?"

One button controls all the windows, in all possible positions. Another can tilt the seats in any of fourteen different ways. The steering wheel can be automatically canted in four different positions, and there is a stereo set with speakers on the right and left, front and back. Air conditioning, two map lights (right and left), tachometer—name it, we got it. And every system has a red warning light which signals if things aren't working properly—and if everything lights up, a drogue chute deploys which brings the car to a dead halt.

We recently moved from Houston, Texas, to Maryland. Scott warned everybody that he was going to drive it nonstop. He started at 5 a.m. and drove steadily for twenty-two hours, with no one spelling him at the wheel. If the children wanted a bathroom stop, they had to make it coincide with a gasoline stop.

I know how he is about trips like that, so I took a plane. When I arrived at our new house, Scott and the children were already there. "What took you so long?" he said. He meant it.

Bonanza has broken just about every long-run popularity record on television, and MICHAEL LANDON, *who plays Little Joe Cartwright, is one of the stars who helped the show do it.*

He told me about the unique system he had for taking girls out on dates in his car, before he was old enough to drive.

I ACTUALLY GOT MY FIRST CAR before I had a license. In New Jersey, where we lived, you had to be seventeen. I was only sixteen. I asked my family for a car, but at that age they weren't about to give me one, or let me drive the family car.

I knew a janitor in one of the buildings nearby—we were pals. And I was working. So he lent me the money, and I paid him back out of my paychecks. The car was a 1939 Studebaker Commander, gray with black fenders, and it cost seventy-five dollars. That's about what it was worth too, because it couldn't go faster than twenty-five miles per hour.

My father knew that I was driving the car without a license. But it was one of those situations where he didn't want to look too closely—if he didn't quite see it with both eyes, it didn't exist. My mother was even more naive than he was. Or maybe more sophisticated. One day it was snowing, so I drove right up to the house. Usually I parked around the corner, or down the street—so as not to force my family to see what I was up to. Anyway, this day it snowed, and I didn't want to walk through it. I had a car, didn't I? And just as luck would have it, there was my mother standing out in front of our house, having a friendly conversation with our local policeman. And she innocently asks him if I could possibly get into trouble for driving when I was underage.

So that was it—I had to put the car in a garage. And it certainly was a cramp at first with the girls—they had become used to me taking them out in my car. But I had a good idea, and I began treating the car as a kind of drive-in. I'd go on the bus to pick up my date, and then we'd take another bus to the garage. Then we'd sit in the car and play the radio. (I'd get the battery charged when it ran down, and bring it back and forth in a paper sack on the bus too.) It really was just like a drive-in without a picture—just the feeling of the two of you in the privacy of the car, and the music playing.

And you know what? The girls all liked the idea. Around our way it became a very popular form of dating.

Courtship and the car—a 1961 cover by Dick Sargent honored the drive-in that gave kids with cars (and broad-minded parents) someplace new to go.

NANCY FRIDAY, *author of the novel,* How To Be Annie, *talks about cars and sexual awakenings.*

I GREW UP IN A STATE where you got your driving license at fourteen. The timing of the license just happened to coincide with the dawning of our awareness of the boys we had grown up with, played with and fought with. Suddenly, curiously, frighteningly, now we saw them as "boys"—the opposites. Now, when we saw them, there were funny wavelengths, everybody wanting both to touch and to run away. The car helped solve this dilemma for us.

Since school was over at 2 p.m., we had the whole afternoon with nothing to do. Up till then we had spent those afternoons at sports or sitting in the movies seeing double features and eating cream puffs. Now cream puffs caused pimples, and besides, there was suddenly something more amusing to do.

It was called "find the boys." Immediately after school, whoever's turn it was to ask her mother if she could borrow the family car, would. Then she'd pick up the other half-dozen girls, and we would cruise, looking for the familiar cars of the boys. Once spotted, we would immediately turn around and go in the opposite direction. As the boys had been looking for us, we were naturally spotted, and followed. The chase was on.

Where were we headed? Nowhere. What were we running from? We didn't know. Suddenly, when we decided to stop, it was ostensibly to watch the basket-

Courtship and the car—three views from ads. Below, whispering sweet nothings about the superiority of the 1931 Buick.

Double-dating in a 1929 Chevrolet. Note plate on top of the rear fender; you stepped there while climbing (gracefully, you hoped) into the rumble seat. Below, honeymooning (note old shoe) in a 1913-model car. If American-made, it was one of the last with steering wheel on the right (wrong) side.

ball game at the playground, but actually to accost one another. We would look at the boys, a few remarks (hilarious) would be exchanged, some boy might playfully hit a girl who was teasing him. The air would become charged, we would pile back in our respective cars, and the chase would be on again. The cars brought us together, but also kept us separate and intact. They let us get to know the opposite sex without letting us become too frightened.

On Friday nights, after dancing class, we had our first dates. Alone with a boy in the car, there was a sense of submission, of excitement and of anxiety. For it was in the car that the first kisses were exchanged and a girl had to decide how far she wanted to go. There was an awful lot of weighty decision-making in those cars, and when a girl advanced toward her dates, she did so with a certain anticipation and fear.

I think, even today, for most grown girls and women, that there is a sexual connotation about the car. Even now, when I get in a car with another man . . . not the man to whom I'm married . . . I still feel a certain zing inside at the *thunk* of the door.

JOSEPH PAPALEO, *author of the novel*, All the Comforts, *teaches English and creative writing at Sarah Lawrence College. We walked across the early spring-green lawns, and he told me about his father's car—and T.S. Eliot.*

IN 1931 my father was the richest man in our little Italian enclave in the Bronx. Since everybody else had a house and seemed to be eating as much as we did, he accepted the suggestion of my older brothers that we buy a car. He purchased a Buick, with shades on the windows and little glass vases in which we kept fresh lilies of the valley and other flowers from our garden.

My brothers learned how to drive first, and then took my father out to the untraveled roads of the far East Bronx to teach him. The first night they returned, I remember sitting in the kitchen as my father came in and sat down in his chair like a man who had just been through a battle. My brothers stood near and waited for him to speak. He waited a long time before he said, "I can't do it."

My brothers tried to reassure him. Sure you can, Pop. It just takes a few more lessons. You have to get used to the road, the steering, the shifting.

But no, my father was certain he could never do it. I was surprised because he was a very strong man, and a brave one, who had emigrated alone as a boy of sixteen, worked his way through school, and had become a very successful clothing designer. I was always very happy when I could visit his office and see his name, which was mine, too, on three glass doors in gold letters.

As he drank the coffee my mother made, he began to explain. "The car goes too fast," he said, and when my brothers said he could run it as slowly as he wanted, he went on: "My mind does not have the speed of it. I cannot think as fast as the car. It gets ahead of me all the time. And then I am sure I cannot stop it. Something in me does not believe I will stop, because I am still catching up to the moving ahead."

It was only many years later, while reading T.S. Eliot defending his new poetry—explaining that he could not write in the rhythms of the past because he had grown up with the sound of the locomotive rather than the carriage—that I realized what my father was trying to say. Growing up in the mountains of Calabria had made him strong and brave—but never prepared him for the pace of the automobile. He just did not have its speed and rhythm inside him.

Up to his very last years he avoided cars, but then the tax situation created the company car, and Poppas was driven into work each morning. I remember asking him how he liked it. "It's quiet," he said, "and I see the river and the bridges every morning." He fingered the handlebar moustache he still wore. "But no. It all goes too fast."

High-powered automobiles made Americans kings of the road. Some found the potential frightening; more loved it. On this page, a 1930 ad for pistons. Opposite, a 1919 ad for tires.

WALTER CRONKITE, *the anchor man on the CBS News team, is also a racing driver and has driven in many important sports-car races. But during a recent visit in his office, he told me this story about the everyday driver, out in the family car*—the demon.

ONE AFTERNOON I was walking along the street, thinking of a dinner party I was going to that night. As it happened, I had not yet met my host. A tie caught my eye in a store window, and I bought it, thinking I might wear it that night. I was standing at the corner, taking another look at it, when the light changed in my favor, and I began to cross the street. And suddenly, rushing the light he had already missed, came a demon driver. I was in the right—my light was green. But he had a couple of tons of steel on his side. He forced me to jump back, brushing me so close that the tie package was knocked to the road and run over by his rear wheels. He careened around the corner on two wheels, spraying me with mud from a puddle. I was mad enough to fix the car in my memory, a blue-and-white four-door sedan with a dent in the right front door.

At the dinner party that night, I told the story. It was my belief, I said, that it is the anonymity of the man in the car that gives him such a feeling, almost of arrogance, toward the man on foot. "He's got this sense of secret, overwhelming power," I said.

"That's right," said my host, who taught biology at the local university. He was happily married, father of three handsome boys, and a very attentive host. He poured my wine when he saw I might like a little more, offered me cigarettes, subtly steered the conversation toward topics he felt might interest me. "That's right," he said. "The man in the car may be marvelous if you meet him socially, in everyday circumstances. But in his car he can get away with things he would never dream of pulling in his living room. Because he *can* get away with it. All he has to do is step on the gas." All this led easily and naturally into an interesting conversation about just how civilized most of us happen to be, after all.

When it came time to go, I found my own car wouldn't start. Our host, hearing the sick whine of my engine, came out, and with the perfect courtesy I had become accustomed to during the evening at his house, insisted that he would drive me to my hotel. He opened his garage door, and backed out. As you've probably guessed, he had a blue-and-white car, and as I opened the front door to get in, I saw that it was dented. He hadn't even recognized himself in my story.

Power, speed, change. Here, a 1931 ad for pistons. Opposite, a Post *cover calling attention to the first showing of 1940 models.*

Speaking of Autos

By Prominent Americans, 1968

Dr. Milton S. Eisenhower
President-Emeritus of Johns Hopkins University.

About 1905, when I was a small boy in Abilene, Kansas, a family living near us purchased one of the first automobiles in town. Every kid in town came to see this mechanical marvel. We knew it was a fascinating ve-

hicle but didn't dream of the many ways it would change our lives and the face of America.

At that time country towns such as Abilene were largely isolated. Young people didn't know the whole country as they do today. The railroad was our route to the outer world, and I well remember my first trip, when I was in high school, to Kansas City, Missouri, 150 miles away. I was scared to death to be going so far away from home.

When I look back, it seems incredible that so many far-reaching advances could have come in my lifetime. In education we saw the one-room country school disappear as students were transported by bus to larger, better-staffed consolidated schools. And right now the mobility of people is playing an important part in adult education. At Johns Hopkins University approximately 7,500 students are enrolled in night classes, and some of them drive to the campus from as far as 50 miles away. Within a relatively few years probably half our college students will be commuting to school.

I suspect that this country's love affair with the automobile has been a major influence in causing us to become such a technology-minded people. The car has done much to build an understanding and feeling for machines, and an appreciation of what can be accomplished by research. When I was a youngster there wasn't a single industrial research laboratory in the country. Yet today we have a broad-based technological development, constantly refreshed by scientific research which enables the United States to produce 37 percent of the world's goods with only 7 percent of the world's population.

Had we realized what a fantastic impact the automobile would have on where and how we live, work and play, we no doubt would have done a better job of planning ahead. But on the whole we really haven't done badly. Our early emphasis on farm-to-market highways was an essential part of the agricultural revolution that made it possible for fewer and fewer farmers to produce all the food and fiber the nation requires. Our national highways—and our still-incomplete interstate network—have helped bring about the marvelous decentralization of industry and development of the interior of our country.

RALPH McGILL
Publisher, the Atlanta Constitution.

THROUGH THE YEARS I have watched the Fords become one of the factors that changed the South, and of course the nation. A demand came for roads. And when the roads were better, the small towns began to suffer. Trade went with the Fords to the larger towns. The automobile was one of the forces that has made a new environment for man. The mobility of the American people is probably the greatest phenomenon of the 20th century. The automobile did that.

I remember the scenes at southern county seats during court weeks and in the squares of towns where the long lines of cotton wagons stood waiting their turn at the gin. The squares would be a mixture of wagons, buggies and Fords. In the cotton towns the Fords would arrive with cotton lint caught in the edges of the hood and on other portions of the old Lizzies. Families would come to town on Saturdays to shop—six and eight, grandma, grandpa, mother, father and the kids, all packed somehow into the faithful old Lizzie. Once, they had gone as a family group in wagons with straight chairs placed in rows.

Men understood the uncomplicated Lizzie. Her four cylinders were not complex. She could be "fixed" with wire and pliers. New parts were few and easily obtainable.

Today men have pride in their big costly cars, shining wonders of technology. But rare is the man who knows what is wrong when his automobile stops or develops trouble. The old man-to-car relationship has been gone a long, long time.

John M. Culkin, S.J.
Director, Center for Communications, Fordham University.

I'M NOT particularly interested in automobiles as such. I'm much more concerned with the self-perception our young people have, in the values and lifestyles which make them people or non-people. Today's mobility of youth assists them in becoming self-directed people. Parents and church and school no longer have a monopoly on what kids learn. The young can break out and look at the world in new ways and interact with it. That really is a fantastic change.

This doesn't just mean love-making in the back seat of a car. It applies to everything. In the old days everything was set out for young people. All of their roles were assigned within the static walled city, the small town, the suburbs—within a this-is-the-way-we-do-things-around-here mentality.

People should feel integral with their world—and it is very hard for today's kids to feel integral with the world of their parents. That world has about had it. It was tidy. It was a world of sensory deprivation. Don't touch. Don't move around. Everything has its place. That world did violence to human beings.

Today's mobility enables young people to break out from a static society. It makes their responses and their behavior depend on themselves, not just on whether or not their old man is around. That mobility is part of the current unrest among young people. They don't want to be labeled, put in pigeonholes—always bad things. Now the kids have an alternative. With a car a youngster can just split, head out, and all the people who have

power over him have less power when he is outside the reach of their radar screen.

Take a youngster going to one of those antiseptic, factorylike schools. When he walks into that polyethylene culture, there is no place for the soul to grab. The values and styles are all 19th-century stuff that the teachers are trying to pass on to the kids, what the mothers want them to learn. But now the youngster can leave that environment, take off his shoes, get in his car, put the top down and let the wind bang at him, let music bang out at him, feel the road under his wheels. He probably couldn't put the words on it, but he feels that he is his own human being.

Lewis Mumford
Author and social philosopher.

THE AUTOMOBILE has its place, but it should not be all over the place. We need a complex network of many forms of transportation—rail, air, water and roadway —each serving the other, each moving at its own pace.

Unhappily, we have dedicated our civic efforts to serving automobile traffic at the expense of nearly every other human need. We have come to look upon the automobile as a religion, and like every other religion, the cult of the motorcar demands its sacrifices. The hearts of many of our great cities have been gouged out to make way for expressways, parking lots and garages.

Youth and the automobile. Three views by Post *cover artists Stevan Dohanos, George Hughes and (opposite page) Norman Rockwell. The years these covers appeared: 1953, 1961, 1954.*

Less obvious but equally debilitating is the financial tribute we pay to the automobile and its servant industries. We are taxed brutally to build the highways that disperse us from one dull suburb to another equally dull suburb, but we suffer shamefully from overburdened schools, inadequate police, overcrowded recreation areas, poorly staffed hospitals and ill-supported libraries.

The answer? First, a process of miniaturization. For high-speed travel between cities the family-size car has many advantages. For town use we must insist upon a car that fits the city's need. What we need is a vehicle even smaller than the smallest compact, a true mini-car that might carry no more than two passengers.

We must also replan our inner cities for pedestrian circulation, and rebuild and extend our public transportation. In our enchantment with the motorcar, we have forgotten that the most flexible, most efficient means for moving short distances is by foot. We have also forgotten that rail transportation can move as many as 50,000 people per hour along a two-track route. In the same time the best expressways can move approximately one tenth that number. There are hopeful signs. More cities are refurbishing their long-neglected rapid-transit systems. More are creating pedestrian malls at their central core. Americans, caught up in the jogging craze, are beginning to regain the use of their legs. This is a very good thing—if in time it will teach us to treat the walking man with that honor and respect we now accord only to the motorcar.

JOHN KENNETH GALBRAITH
Economist and former Ambassador to India.

I HAVE DRIVEN an automobile off and on since I was old enough to hold the wheel, and I have found them very useful. I have always been under the impression that anything that was good for me was probably good for other people too. Anything that lifts us out of our narrow and instinctive parochialism is a good thing, and certainly nothing has moved people beyond the horizons as has the automobile.

On the other hand it is not an unmitigated blessing. Among other things there can be no question that the

automobile brings with it the world's most hideous architecture. A great many people have criticized the automobile for its bizarre design, but nobody has really paid any attention to the absolutely dreadful architecture that is associated with it.

Nothing has so drastically damaged the American scene as the service station. Not only is it designed by architects whose sole motivation is to be competitively hideous, but the people who maintain them put up meaningless flags and pennants, and distribute about the premises discarded parts of vehicles and used paper cups and empty bottles—a comprehensive display of all the trash that modern civilization accumulates. It would be hard to imagine how anything could be better designed to desecrate both town and country.

In time we will have to zone long stretches of our roads against the detritus of an automobile civilization; not only service stations but hot-dog stands and pizza stands and all the shabbier roadside commerce that the automobile creates. The places of rest and assignation that it encourages along the road, often called motels, leave something to be desired too. It is not beyond reason that we shall eventually have to set minimum standards of architecture, appearance and cleanliness for all such places of public accommodation.

Since I always buy the simplest car that will provide transportation, I pay little attention to obsolescence engendered by stylistic changes. If the automobile industry is bamboozling people into buying a new car

merely because the old one looks out of date, those who fall for this gambit are suffering from their wealth rather than their poverty. One can't feel terribly sorry for them.

Of course, there is the argument that it is necessary to create this desire for a new car every year just to keep this great production machine going, to keep men at work. If we have to artifice a society in which the basic mechanism is the creation of work in order to work, then we are in rather poor condition, cars or no cars. Maybe we should drive old cars longer and put in less energy building them. Maybe one day we will.

Hopefully, over time, we will stabilize the number of people making automobiles. We can't go on covering more and more of the country with the automobile and its accessory construction, and we have already seen what disintegrative effect it has on the city. This is the greatest social impact of the automobile. It gave people a choice between improving the city as a household in which to live, or escaping from it. At least it gives the wealthy and the middle class that choice, and most of them opted out, leaving the central city to the poor and the black, to those who could not afford a car.

Problems and progress. On the opposite page, an intercity bus of 1930 and a 1928 traffic jam (there were already complaints about unsightly roadside billboards). Here, a 1930 family bravely ignores gathering clouds to join in a "Salute to Motordom," while a 1954 family, painted by Post *cover artist Thornton Utz, succeeds in renting the last unit in a nearly full motel.*

PHILIP HAMMER
President, American Society of Planning Officials.

THE AUTOMOBILE is not the villain that many city planners assume it to be. Surely it is responsible to a great degree for the creation of outlying shopping centers, those nodes around which cities in miniature arise on the periphery of the old town. Much of this decentralization is quite legitimate. Even if we had discovered, through some stroke of genius, how to get downtown fast and easily, it would hardly have been wise to continue piling up businesses there, one on top of another.

But it is clear now that the satellite areas that have spun off from the central city have begun to experience their own problems of congestion. It will not be enough, therefore, to concern ourselves only with the old downtown, nor even with the city plus the peripheral areas. A transportation pattern embracing the entire region must be worked out, one in which the automobile meshes with various forms of mass transit —rail and highway, surface and underground. The main objective is simply this: to move people from place to place as quickly, easily, cheaply and safely as possible, by whatever means can do the job best.

ROBERT MOSES
Former Chairman of the Triborough Bridge Authority, New York City.

THOUGH MY LIFE INTEREST has been in the roads and parkways over which the automobile travels rather than in the vehicle itself, I do have certain views on the motorcar as an instrument of social change. To me it is not the be-all and end-all of our civilization, the crowning product of our genius. It is a form of transportation. The last automobile that I personally owned and drove was a Model T Ford, and I have not been uncritical of the cars that Detroit has produced since that time. The automobile of today is too elaborate—too long, too wide, too cluttered up with gadgets that are both expensive and unnecessary. Above all, it is overpowered. The advertising of speed and the building for speed are thoroughly bad things in my book. Speed is and always has been the great enemy of highway safety.

At the same time I do not share the views of some of our more vociferous social critics that the automobile is responsible for all the ills that afflict the cities. It is the temper of the times to blame the motorcar for all urban blight and urban sprawl and urban congestion. This is idiocy. Every form of transport, from the oxcart to the airplane, has resulted in both the dispersal and the concentration of populations, and every traveled route, from the Roman road to the expressway, has had the same effect. The automobile did not create man. Man created the automobile, and whatever blight and ugliness can be blamed on the car is man-made and in great degree could have been avoided.

Much could be done, for example, to relieve the congestion that now hampers traffic movement in the areas of high density. One of the simplest and most effective ways would be to regulate the size and movement of trucks. Think what a difference it would make if you could put through a rule that certain kinds of heavy trucking could take place only at night.

Above all, we need not accept the idea that the roads the automobile travels on must inevitably blight the surrounding landscape. I've never had any patience with the idea that you had to blast and bulldoze your way from point to point by the shortest route.

Trucks and tourists. A 1932 offering of Chevrolet's six-cylinder commercial vehicles, and a 1936 drive through Yosemite.

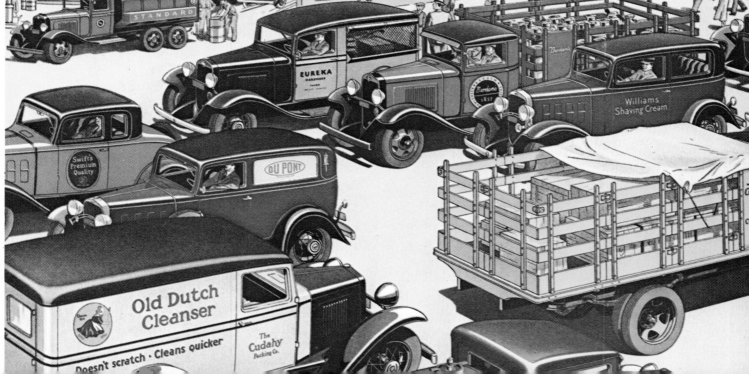

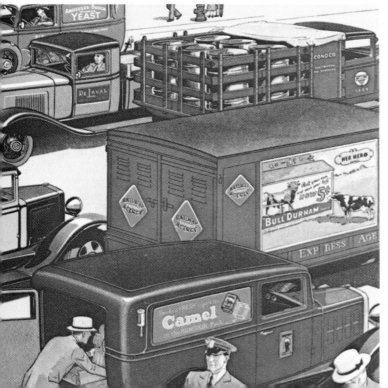

ERIC SEVAREID
Commentator for the Columbia Broadcasting System.

DRIVING FOR PLEASURE now is practically a thing of the past in this country. In England you still see old ladies out in their cars for a Sunday drive, looking at the buttercups. But not here—there is just too much traffic.

Much of our countryside is still alive and real and full of nature. But for how long? Many of our places of great natural beauty—our lakes, mountains and seashores—are becoming so accessible that they are being ruined by sheer numbers and bad taste. Our parks are being covered by beer cans. Perhaps we should have a rule about roads to our still-wild places: Don't pave them. Make it tough to get there. Then perhaps only those people who really appreciate such country will put up with the hardship of going there.

The Auto in Our Lives 151

Only yesterday we had technology tamed and made cozy. (A 1952 Post *cover by Stevan Dohanos.)*

BUCKMINSTER FULLER
Engineer-Inventor whose many creations include the Dymaxion three-wheeled, streamlined vehicle.

I FIND the automobile completely misunderstood.

The automobile has had a great impact on humanity, but it is *not* an investment. It is *not* a way to earn a living. It is *not* just a modernized buggy with an engine in place of a horse.

Rather, the car is an important part in the continuing evolution in which man is learning to master energy. This ability has altogether changed our ecology, our relationship to our total environment.

We have learned some of the principles of energy only in recent times. For much of his history, man used energy only in an empirical way. He couldn't take energy from the sun through his skin; only vegetation can do that. But he could eat the animals that eat the grass. As a hunter he got enough energy that way.

When man became a farmer, he began to use buildings to store and handle energy. When I look at the early farmstead, I see many buildings—barns, granaries, corncribs, icehouses, woodsheds. These helped the

farmer to keep his food preserved, some things cold, some dry, some cooked, some wet. All these are chemical conditions of energy.

After man developed energy machines, such as the steam engine and the electric generator, he began to bring controlled energy into his house. The refrigerator took the place of the icehouse, the oil furnace and electric stove the place of the woodshed. Machines in the home gave us heat and cold, cleaned our skin and our clothes, preserved our food and took the place of servants.

Now the automobile really started as part of the house—the front porch or the parlor. In early days young people courted in the front parlor—and then people began to have time to sit on front porches, to visit with neighbors there, to enjoy the view. Many glazed in the front porch so they could sit there on winter days.

Then, in effect, we put wheels under the front porch, put an engine in it and took off down the street. The kids began to explore the world, spending less and less time around home. Up to the time of my father the average distance covered in a lifetime was about 30,000 miles. I have already covered 3.5 million miles, 100 times as far. The important thing is that the car enabled the kids to start exploring the world, and they learned that the people in the next town or the next state weren't necessarily savages, as they had been told.

As a social force, the automobile has been magnificent. It has broadened the horizon of humanity. It has helped man get rid of some of his inferiority complex: Where once only the king rode in the coach and the rest of us were servants, suddenly all could ride. It has taught man to make some judgments and think a little farther ahead. It opened up the whole age of mass production and mass consumption.

But *now* we have to think beyond the automobile age—and in a big way. We are masters enough of energy today to travel in *multidimensionality*. With the automobile we are using only the linear direction; we have everybody going through a tube, in effect, moving in opposite directions at 65 or 70 miles an hour, with the two lines of traffic only a few feet apart. What kind of nonsense is that? We have millions of people spending hours steering down highways in streams of cars. They might as well be on a track.

Yet we have four dimensions, including frequency, in which to travel. We have all of space at our command. What I see coming is this: When you wish to go somewhere, you will put on a simple harness, something like a vest, with jet stilts that go under your arms like crutches. You will simply step to the door, dial the beam you plan to travel on, and off you go, at great speed. By the time the next person takes off, you will be miles away. In multidimensionality the amount of free space is fantastically great.

Buckminster Fuller foresees a post-automobile world of multidimensionality, but we will fight it. We Americans will fight to the death for our flower beds and picket fences, and for parking space at the curb for the family car.

"Hell Creek Crossing" by William Faulkner is from *The Reivers*. Copyright © 1962 by William Faulkner. Reprinted by permission of Random House, Inc.

"Gatsby's Party" by F. Scott Fitzgerald is from *The Great Gatsby*. Copyright 1925 Charles Scribner's Sons. Reprinted with the permission of Charles Scribner's Sons.

Except for the selections by Erma Bombeck and F. Scott Fitzgerald, all text reprinted here first appeared in *The Saturday Evening Post*. Copyright © 1902, 1903, 1915, 1916, 1918, 1919, 1922, 1926, 1928, 1930, 1931, 1932, 1933, 1934, 1937, 1946, 1954, 1962, 1966, 1967, 1968, 1976 The Curtis Publishing Company. The editors wish to thank the authors and their heirs and agents who have graciously cooperated with us in the republication of this material.

ILLUSTRATIONS

Photo sources: Page 6—Brown Brothers; 7, 10—Culver Pictures, Inc.; 11—The Bettmann Archive; 18, 29, 30—Brown Brothers; 31, 34—Culver Pictures, Inc.; 42, 43—Brown Brothers; 54—

1929 Reo

Culver Pictures, Inc.; 59, 60, 61, 79 (bottom), 89—Brown Brothers; 95—The Bettmann Archive; 113, 114, 115, 117—Brown Brothers; 118 (top)—The Ford Motor Company; 118 (bottom)—Brown Brothers; 125 (bottom)—The Chrysler Corporation; 126 (top)—General Motors; 148 (bottom)—Brown Brothers.

With the exception of historical photographs that appear on the pages listed above, all illustrations in this book are reproduced from the pages of *The Saturday Evening Post*. Copyright © 1902, 1903, 1905, 1906, 1907, 1908, 1911, 1912, 1913, 1914, 1915, 1916, 1917, 1918, 1919, 1920, 1922, 1923, 1925, 1926, 1927, 1928, 1929, 1930, 1931, 1932, 1933, 1934, 1936, 1937, 1939, 1940, 1944, 1947, 1949, 1952, 1953, 1954, 1956, 1957, 1958, 1959, 1960, 1961, 1968 The Curtis Publishing Company.

Dates following the author's name or at the end of a selection indicate when the material first appeared in print.

Acknowledgments

TEXT

"The Second-Car Ten-Day War" by Erma Bombeck is from *The Grass Is Always Greener Over the Septic Tank*. Copyright © 1975 by Erma Bombeck. Used with permission of McGraw-Hill Book Company.

KAISER

Maxwell

CHEVROLET

BODY by FISHER

Packard

DODGE BROTHERS

Studebaker

PAIGE
The Standard of Value and Quality

REO

AVBVRN

CHRYSLER PLYMOUTH

Hupmobile

Buick

Ford

CHALMERS · MOTOR · CO
CMC
Detroit, Mich. U.S.A.
Quality First

Overland

DURANT

CADILLAC

OLDSMOBILE
PRODUCT OF GENERAL MOTORS